WARNING:

YOU CANNOT *THINK* LIKE A MAN IF YOU ARE NOT A MALE.

There are authors in the marketplace that will lead you to believe that a woman can mirror the thoughts and logic of men by performing certain acts, or knowing certain warning signs.

Truth of the matter, these are people who have concocted a series of manipulative techniques and essentially, are training women in how to "persuade" individuals to perform their bidding. It is impossible for a woman to "think like a man, and act like a lady". Not only is this statement irresponsible, juvenile and unrealistic, in my opinion, it implies "acting", deceptively behaving a particular way and therefore, sets the stage for a larger issue later.

This book isn't like that. I thought perhaps women would like to know what it is we think about them, their kids, the relationships, etc. I thought instead of writing the stuff Black men would like our women to do, I would write and tell women what men *really* think about our counterparts and our interaction with them.

Like me, most of these authors seem to be people who have done more than the average in the way of romance. Most of us seem to be experienced in bed-hopping, deception, and manipulation. Having "been around the block" as they say, we writers all seem to have made the same mistakes over and over and are attempting to spare others the pain and heartache that we brought on ourselves.

Others who are more complacent with their lifestyles and quality of life create "how-to" manuals for those eager to see what it's like and how the "other half" live. These people measure themselves by material possessions and their ability to exploit others. If you weren't sophisticated enough to see through their façade, the fault rests with you and your powers of perception, not the charlatan that commits the fraud.

In my opinion, whenever someone suggests that they have the fool-proof, sure-fire method for having a healthy committed relationship, I never had to look further than the source of the advice and usually my first question: what does their life look like?

Another question: how can someone who has been divorced repeatedly give me advice on *keeping* a relationship?

I realize there are people who will gain insight after a stressful and trying situation, and, can shed light on the many emotional pitfalls to avoid and so on, but, when you consider these people have failed repeatedly, yet are convinced they have it figured out, something doesn't seem quite right.

Not to mention the fact, the person allegedly stole the idea anyway

Maybe it's just me that feels that way.

This collection of words can be considered a manifesto of sorts. I intended it to be part social commentary, and part political satire inspired by some personal experiences and insights drawn from them. Although, I am hardly an expert on relationships, I have come to some conclusions that can be applicable in many different scenarios. There may be portions that will irritate, inflame, enrage even the most liberal of minds, but, if considered objectively, hopefully all who peruse the content herein will be thoroughly entertained, as I attempted to extend a little wisdom through humor.

In laymen's terms: fucking relax and check out what I wrote, and when you're finished, I challenge you to say there isn't one thing in this book that could apply to you.

INTRODUCTION

When I had the idea to write a book to women explaining the male perspective, I tried to consider the possible backlash. If the book is successful enough, no doubt there will be some feminist group or irate women in general that will be opposed to it. I'm sure my yahoo accounts will get flooded with e-mails and personal instant messages from all the women that will insist that the things I wrote don't apply to them. To be completely honest, when I consider the possible negative backlash, I expect the worst. I'm actually looking forward to it, I hope for it, I WANT IT!!

Why?

It opens the door for dialogue between the sexes. The market is over-run with how to manuals, relationship guides, and books on every conceivable situation and what one should do to improve their chances of attracting and keeping a mate. I have seen books written by former and current pimps detailing how to be an effective philanderer. There are numerous websites and pages dedicated to teaching men how to play 'the game."

In essence, these authors profit by selling dreams of sex, romance, and newfound confidence to the lonely, self-conscious, and desperate. Ironically, many of these same authors have experienced one failed relationship after another, so the thought of these people advising others in the ways of love, to me is laughable.

This book isn't that.

After a one of my many long profanity laced rants, a woman asked me; "why do you have to call that woman a bitch?"

I didn't have an answer.

Beyond the fact that was the first word that came to mind, I really didn't know why I called women bitches. I always thought there was a general definition of what a bitch was; contrary, argumentative, bossy, combative, disagreeable, selfish, un-cooperative. Perhaps it was the way that the word had become common, it's in music, movies, television programs, on t-shirts.

Bitch is everywhere.

Its funny when you hear it in certain phrases, "I'm

rich, bitch!" as made famous by Dave Chappelle. Point is, everyone in the Black community seems to have a different take on the word. Some Black women use it towards each other as a term of endearment, yet still get highly offended if men use it.

Riding bitch is a term that refers to being a passenger on a motorcycle.

"Ain't that a bitch?" is a phrase that is meant to express surprise, shock, or disbelief.

The word bitch has many different meanings, but for the most part, it is meant to convey a feeling of contempt for someone else. In the penal system, it means weakness: a man is a "bitch" when he is the willing and usually passive participant in a forced homosexual relationship.

All those things aside, when I really sat and considered why I called Black women "bitches", I realized it was because of attitudes, behaviors, and the fact I had been programmed to. Unknowingly, I had assimilated to popular belief, I thought words only had the impact of the context in which they were used, but I soon learned the error in my thinking.

Everyone interprets differently, what may have been intended as a harmless poke, could escalate into a full blown brawl, if someone mishears a word, or mistranslates a statement. I have seen people killed over simple misunderstandings because no-one was interested in hearing the other persons side once anger was introduced to the situation.

Every time I said or called someone the word bitch, I had a general definition in mind that I was referring to, one that I shared with many Black men. Problem is, the definition we use isn't the one Black women hear when they interpret the word.

The best way to articulate our definition of the word is to detail the perspective of the average Black man. In this book I will attempt to explain to Black women some of the reasons behind Black men's attitudes and behavior. I cannot presume I speak for every Black man, but I'm confident when I assert I know most of them will relate to what I wrote.

This book is not a weak attempt to justify any negative behavior, but rather, a sincere expose of the things many Black men feel but cannot express.

In simpler terms:

This is why we call you bitch.

EVEN STEVEN HAWKING IS BAFFLED

There have been many people throughout history that were labeled "brilliant, talented, influential, or great thinkers". In many cases these were the people responsible for the advances in technology, music and the arts, medicine, science, philosophy, politics, etc. When one thinks of physics, is it not almost natural to conjure images of Albert Einstein, wild haired and wide eyed, with a look similar to a deer caught in headlights?

Confined to a wheelchair, communicating through a computer keypad with a digitized voice simulator, it would be easy to overlook Mr. Hawking as just another handicapped man. Steven Hawking is much like Einstein; his theories are praised, quoted, and regarded as absolute truth by his devoted supporters and admirers of his work.

As a theoretical physicist, his conclusions have enraged, enlightened, and encouraged his colleagues, as he has postulated on everything from the big bang, to the existence of life in distant galaxies. His theories have brought him praise and ridicule from the scientific community, as well as numerous parodies and comedic sketches, where he has been portrayed as everything from frail genius to emotionally detached womanizer.

Suffice it to say, this is a well-known, smart man. Imagine how shocked I was to find out the one mystery this intellectual giant cannot crack is the riddle of what the hell will make a woman happy. Yet, on January 5, 2012 as reported by Reuters, when asked what he thinks about most, Hawking replied, "Women. They are a complete mystery." This is the guy who made many contributions to understanding the UNIVERSE and HE doesn't get women? So, what about the rest of us, we who lack the mental faculties to comprehend the complexities of black holes, m-theory, or any of the associated sciences, what chance in hell we do we have of conquering our confusion when dealing with the opposite sex?

Although I write with a tone of sarcasm, in my opinion, there is a subliminal yet pervasive fear of never understanding women that all men share. This fear is one of many determining factors in our behavior, although many men will never admit it.

Many times we find ourselves acting irrationally because of this fear, resulting in debt, loss, violence and sadly sometimes even death. It is my conclusion that this combination of ignorance, ego fueled machismo and fear is the primary reason why we call you bitches, hoes, tramps, sluts, cunts, and so on.

I am by no means trying to justify the use of the aforementioned insults, rather I try to give an explanation of what would motivate a male, who was birthed by a woman, or may have female relatives, use words that are detestable to all women. My intention is to share with the reader a compilation of viewpoints shared by Black men that I have encountered over the years, in the hopes that by exposing some of the myths and misconceptions to open the platform for a dialogue and ultimately, some kind of reconciliation between genders within the Black community.

MOMMY AND RESPECT

It is common knowledge that a large majority of Black men in the world today have been raised in a fatherless household. This fact, I believe, is one the main components of the problem.

As I have seen reflected in the maternal instinct, most mothers are naturally inclined to keep her family together, and as the sole provider for the family unit, she was more predisposed to worry as she often had to "rob Peter to pay Paul" as it were for her tribes essential needs. This usually resorted in a sort of cloaked anxiety and the approach that if things didn't put food on the table or pay a bill, then it wasn't important, relevant, or even practical. I personally believe this is why interest in the arts, especially classical music has all but disappeared. Black folk "have better things to do" than sit around plucking a string or hitting a key.

As a result of this, I believe, our culture has been the biggest victim.

Black men have been taught to fear everything.

Most mothers, well-meaning and otherwise, have unconsciously reinforced their sons with fear of exploration , abandonment, and commitment. Any endeavor that one engages in is supposed to produce a profit, satisfy an impulse, or control/pacify any would be debate.

"Get your education so you can get a good job and find a good woman."

Meaning: a degree will make you all the more desirable.

This is just a general example of the many different mind-fucks men have thrust upon them from childhood. One should never pursue a career or field of study that he enjoys or is interested in, he should just apply for the one that has the highest earning potential.

This is destructive on so many levels.

Consider the person who has been encouraged to become a doctor or lawyer his entire life, only to fail in school because he wasn't naturally adept at science/biology or remembering statues and rulings, or even taught the importance and necessity of the aforementioned subjects in the particular fields to which they apply. The most ironic part, when he tells his parent of his failure, its usually met with ridicule and disgust, which destroys what's left of his already damaged psyche.

"You weren't trying hard enough."

"You must be dumb or something."

Even if she's wrong, you can't get mad at momma…because, she's momma.

The truth is, "Momma" is the first woman we ever learn to love. Most men usually are attracted to, date, and marry women who resemble, or remind them of their mothers, sometimes apparent sometimes subconsciously.

Most men have been taught to cater to women under all circumstances. Women are to be respected at all times, even at the expense of a man's dignity or self -respect. I have stated before that I believe most women teach their sons to be the men they would have liked to date. These same men are conditioned to believe they are better than their peers because of where they were raised, where they were schooled, their possessions, etc.

Essentially, these men become subconsciously effeminate in ways, overly emotional, hyper sensitive, mental cases, walking around expecting something from everyone.

I wonder how many disillusioned men approached a woman from this distorted, entitled mind-state to have his ego destroyed? Mommy said you were special so you think everyone else agrees.

The relationship between Black mothers and sons is difficult to explain. One could argue that as a result of slavery and racism the Black community has been affected psychologically. Perhaps seeing their parents, mates, siblings, and children murdered, kidnapped, raped, beaten and humiliated, mothers did what they had to just to ensure the safety of her family.

Prostitution was a means to an end in most cases, and countless women have degraded themselves to save the life of a man threatened because of his skin color. No matter how you explore the origins or the effects of our collective past, the fact is, Black mothers and sons share a bond that transcends the biological and borders on the spiritual.

To me, this is a blessing and a curse.

The love of mother has been the downfall of many a man. The demands for attention or money, likewise, his need of his parents' praise or acknowledgement, have been the undoing of a great number of guys. Failed marriages, unwanted children, bankruptcies, murders and all sorts of atrocities have been committed under the guise of winning mom's approval. We spend a lot of time trying to make our parents proud and rarely do we stop to analyze the negative effects of living life by the demands of others.

HOW CAN YOU KNOW WHO YOU ARE WHEN WE NEVER LEARN OURSELVES?

If you were to traverse cyberspace in search of Black men's opinions on their counterparts, you would no doubt feel assaulted by the variety of perspectives and the passion in which they have been articulated. The countless blogs, videos, songs, and twitter posts all seem to have a common theme, "we are tired of the behaviors/attitudes we get from our women." It's safe to say that many Black men feel minimized, unappreciated, and downright helpless when dealing with "sisters".

These complaints are usually met with disgust, deflections, ridicule, shock, anger, or outright disregard and excuses. It is almost as if some women are incapable of empathizing, or just refuse to. Understanding is not abundant in the Black community. We are a people consumed by our passions, united by our past, yet separated by our own selfish desires.

As a young man, I can't recall how many times I had been admonished to go to school get a trade and "get my learning, so I could take care of a family" as if that was what life was all about. Slaving away for a wage and providing for those dependent on me. In my teens, kids were the last of my worries, so the thought that I had to follow what I saw as a depressing pattern into adulthood, and that would be the pinnacle of my existence didn’t appeal to me. I wanted to travel the world, see the sights, and meet interesting people. I couldn't do that if I were confined to a cubicle or office, or exhausting myself in someone else warehouse. I always knew I didn't want to be anyone's slave.

The most ironic part, the desire to be free, my own

boss, and learned in the things of the world came from my Grandma. It was her insistence that I "shouldn't try to know everything" is what fueled my desire for knowledge.

The world was a puzzle to me and I wanted to figure it out. Who was she to try to limit my knowledge or to plant fear of the unknown in me? All her advice did was galvanize my resolve, and turn me into a voracious reader. I wanted to know everything from the most mundane of trivial facts, to the most complex of philosophies, theories and scientific conclusions.

Why?

Because she said that I shouldn't.

I love my Grandma dearly, as do many people, but knowing her upbringing as a sharecropper and a domestic worker, only having a sixth grade education and having to forge an existence from such humble and meager circumstances, I wondered, why in the hell would she tell me to go to school, but only limit myself to the information that would keep me where she was, submissive, powerless?

I thought parents were supposed to want their kids to do better than them. It made more sense to me become as knowledgeable in as many things as possible, because as they say "knowledge is power", and I wanted to be Superman.

SEX AND ATTRACTION

Let's be honest, in some relationships sex is important. For some unexplained reason we have all been trained to look at sexual situations as taboo or something to be ashamed of, and those who choose to express their sexuality as strange, weird, uncivilized, promiscuous, or downright evil. The popular belief is men are detached emotionally, and incapable of appreciating the delicate nature of intimate encounters. There are many women who believe that most men only live for the conquest, and, a large majority lacks the ability to commit to one woman and remain monogamous.

How many times have you heard the old axiom: "men are dogs"? How about, "well, a man has to be a man"? It is almost as if we have been forced to accept that we are insignificant, sex-crazed buffoons that should feel honored when someone is gracious enough to allow us the privilege of "being with" them. In my opinion this is the root of the problem. The Black community has forgotten how to love.

I have been with a lot of women. There is no other

way to state this fact. I could attempt to glamorize it with some lame cliché that emphasizes the ease in which I manipulated the fairer sex into submitting to my wishes and gratifying some depraved urge I was having. Men always have to convince ourselves that some strange influence that we magically exert is what causes this unknowing damsel to become a willing participant in a passionless unsatisfying tryst with someone undeserving of her attention, much less her affections. But if you were a fly on a wall in a gym or men's room, you would hear some guy bragging about how some woman didn't have a chance against his game.

I really hate when guys do that.

We all have heard some over confident douche bag exhorting the virtues of his animal magnetism, his irresistible charisma, or his limitless resources. For some strange reason, there are legions of men convinced that money is the key to attracting women. There is a new saying common in hip-hop songs these days: IT AIN'T TRICKING IF YOU GOT IT.

What a croc of bullshit.

Tricking is the street slang term for spending frivolously to gain favor with the opposite sex. It originates from the pimp/prostitute street lexicon.

Tricks are what the people who paid for sexual favors were called. You know, the guy spending his entire paycheck at the strip bar in hopes of bagging the dancer he was obsessing over. Or, it could be the passive husband who has to keep his unloving wife living in the lap of luxury. When someone was called a "trick", the assumption was, a little persuasion, some ego stroking, even the promise of a later romantic rendezvous was usually enough to separate the "trick" from his money.

With the surge in popularity in hip-hop in the last decade or so, the materialism that always permeated the recording industry shifted to an environment of even more decadence and perversion. Recreational drug use has increased, not mention the potency of the drugs being imbibed.

What once was the 40 ounce and a blunt society, has been replaced by pill poppin', line snorting, champagne drinking, Facebooking, fashionistas with little to no regard for the future or anyone else. Seems to me, the current social climate of our youth reflects a "DO WHAT THOU WILT" mindstate, originally promoted by occultist Aleister Crowley, and resuscitated by Jay-Z in recent years. It is nothing like the community minded positive music it was in the late eighties/early nineties, now, it's a constant intoxicated orgy, and you're the lame one if you ain't keeping up with the Joneses.

I never really had much in the way of clothing growing up. I was one of those guys who blossomed late. I didn't really come into my own until my late twenties, even then, fashion and trendy clothes were never really that big a deal to me. As soon as you caught wind of the new style then went through the trouble of finding something that was current, something new was in.

So, why even bother?

Sure, I wanted all the designer stuff that I saw the other kids wearing, but since I came from a single alcoholic parent welfare household, that was out of the question.

Well, unless I got a job or stole them.

Tried that….long story for another time.

Point is, its never about the clothes.

It is common knowledge that most women enjoy shopping for, buying, and collecting shoes. There are women so obsessed with footwear, they have more pairs of shoes than they have outfits to go with them. With an endless variety of styles, colors, materials, and uses, you will be hard pressed to find anything else as essential or important to today's woman. I have heard a woman say she will pick a day of shopping for a cute pair of pumps over a man any day.

Keeping this in mind you learn the first rule of appearance.

NEAT AND CLEAN BEATS EXTRAVAGANT AND FLASHY

There are a lot of men that have never learned the rules of fashion. We never had to. If you said to the average Black man, "you know, you can't wear white after labor day", he will probably look at you like you're insane. Tell the average Joe that his belt needs to match his shoes, or that he needs an 1/8" cuff on his trousers, he may respond with "who told you that dumb shit?", or "getthefuckouttahere" which ultimately mean the same thing.

There are no fashion rules in the "hood" "ghetto" or "urban" settings, beyond the two most important ones; no high-water pants, no raggedy shoes. These days men are wearing high end haute couture designer threads and becoming "metrosexuals", materialistic, narcissistic, douche bags, that are embracing that old 80's catchphrase, "It is better to look good than to feel good." Just like Billy Crystal's character Armando was a satire of the shallow materialism of his day, young men these days seem consumed with self-mutilation, and instant gratification more than anything.

I personally don't like today's fashion. There's too many gaudy embellishments, loud colors, and unflattering designs. Everybody looks the same.

Let's explore a thought: In the media, men who are fashion savvy usually fall into one of three categories:

1 The rich playboy. This guy had an awesome wardrobe because he could afford it, and was expected to wear the finest garments and accessories.

2 The artsy/hipster weirdo. It was this guy who had the eclectic taste and took more risks with his fashion choices. If he went against the norm it was accepted because he was "experiencing" life and all of its differences. (yawn.)

3 The sensitive guy of questionable sexual preference. This guy was usually depicted as possibly (or blatantly) homosexual. This individual not only was aware of the newest trends, fabrics, and designers, it was he who ridiculed other men for not being as fine tuned to the beat of what's new hot and current.

Everybody else had to figure it for themselves.

Men are simple animals, especially when it comes to clothes, and most of us hate shopping. After we reach a certain age, clothing becomes optional and only necessary when held in relation to practicality and function.

In other words, if we could go to work, school, weddings and funerals in our favorite sweats and a baseball hat we would, but since we can't, we do enough to get by. Most men have 1 multi-purpose suit, the go to outfit for any formal engagement. Truth is, most men don't know how to match shirts and ties, colors and patterns, designs and fabrics, so why bother? Get something relatively comfortable and keep it as clean as possible. This is common men thinking, and why a lot look like evil villains and goons from really bad b- movies. Good taste in clothes isn't inherited it's taught, and a lot of men never learned.

Women like well-dressed men. This doesn't mean you need a $2000 suit, it means you need to make it look like a $2000 suit. There is an old saying: "It ain't what you wear, it's how you wear it." It can be a warm-up suit, or overalls, the reaction you get from women comes from how you present yourself. A confident man in a clean warm-up suit can say to a woman you're organized, successful and enjoying a day off, mature with a playful side and so on. The main thing is being SELF-ASSURED, being comfortable in your own skin.

There are a lot of women that are moved by materialism and this motivates most men to try to capture a woman's attention with his toys, big mistake.

In my opinion, when a woman assesses your worth by the superficial, it's usually to get a general idea of your finances, and ultimately, what can be spent on her. Since so many men live beyond their means, imagine the confusion that ensues when the would-be gold-digger realizes her meal ticket is really just a bowl of ramen noodles in an expensive bowl.

Several years ago, Jay-Z had a song called "The Power of the Pussy", in which he stated: "that's why we get haircuts and try to dress fly…" which is testament to the mentality that permeates the minds of inner city males. In order to appeal to the opposite sex one only needs to display his best façade, it reminds me of peacocks, heads back, spreading their vibrant plumage and strutting cock-sure to draw attention from the females of the flock.

The reality is, Black men aren't taught about romance or love. We are taught to hypnotize a woman into wanting us.

In the Black community, a "good man" is merely a man obsessed with his wife and or family. Many of us are taught to measure our love for a woman by what we were willing to do for her. Which was mostly; how hard would you work to make sure she was comfortable?

As I have seen with many Black men, the love he has for a woman is reflected in his willingness and ability to cater to his woman. We have heard many a songwriter wax poetic extolling the virtues of love, but beyond the longing for the subject's attention and affections, what else was there? When you look at romanticism in this light, it becomes easier to understand why so many Black men are promiscuous. It becomes a question of "what's in this for me?"

In this light, his job becomes the vessel by which he keeps his world afloat. The job pays the bills, which keeps the woman happy, and, in the house, which means he has a companion/sex partner, which makes sure the kids are cared for and… (add your own sequence same result.)

This is how men become self-imposed slaves. Prisoners in a cell of their own design. His job becomes a burden

As with anything within the human sphere of influence, personal benefit is usually the motivating factor for all parties involved. People tend to forget this. You must remember, the way you are looking for specific traits and behaviors suitable to your happiness, your partner is doing the same, and having things in common doesn't always mean you found your soul-mate.

Men have a tendency for shooting ourselves in the foot, especially when it comes to relationships with women. A lot of us become victims of our own stupidity.

I believe its sheer stupidity that causes some of us to do some of the ridiculous things we do. It starts with a stupid man usually. It's usually some self-absorbed asshole incapable of realizing his faults and adjusting accordingly, some of us would rather blame our mistakes on someone else's ignorance or being ungrateful, when the truth of the matter is: we have been trained to be punks, and no-one seems to see it.

Men also have a tendency to adopt the morals, beliefs, and principals of the woman he's involved with. You know, switch churches, change brands of products, entertainment, etc.

Most men will do anything to keep his woman quiet, happy, and willing to have sex. Unbeknownst to him, this starts a disconnect in the relationship. Once a man begins to compromise the things he enjoys, as many have had to do when entering a committed relationship, it fosters resentment. Why?

He can't be himself.

In some cases, the man has to develop another persona for the sake of his woman. Things that she considers disgusting have to repulse him regardless if he despises them or not.(He likes porn she doesn't) His beliefs sometimes must be modified for sake of keeping the peace, as in situations where the spouse has "gotten saved" or embraced spirituality, going vegan, or is on a diet. Any refusal to participate becomes a glaring admission of selfishness or inability to be supportive.

Why debate when you can just go along with it?

This is the mindset of older Black men, who seemingly in defeat, resign to submitting and allowing his woman to rule the household and relegate himself to role of financial sponsor and disciplinarian. Young Black men see this and shudder at the thought of being treated so disrespectfully, and become resolved to never let a woman "walk all over him" like that old dude..

This leads to the conquer mind-state; it's all about how many women can you seduce and knock-off. How many notches in the belt can you get? The more women you have sex with, the more of a man you are for it. Young Black men are congratulated for and encouraged to get as much sex as he can while he's young, because it's all down-hill after a certain age.

Aging is tantamount to being dead in the Black community; it's almost as if the thinking is, if you're too old to fuck then what good are you? Older men are said to "still have it" if he can attract and bed younger nubile females. It seems that way if you're unfamiliar, the truth is, most of the time, he's throwing his money around, and he lacks the energy to satisfy the woman sexually, so he just supports her financially and reaps the benefits.

In other words…Sugar daddy uses her to look good.

There are way too many men that would rather put on a good show for a night than have to deal with the hopelessness of their lives daily. The Sugar Daddy is an example of this. This guy would rather portray a façade of being cool, strong, virile, hip, so he can seem as if he "still got it" to the younger dudes.

With a lot of the other guys, the strip club, racetrack, casino, friends' houses, or just anywhere other than home becomes a safe haven and a welcome alternative to a miserable home-life resulting from a troubled relationship. No matter how we try to explain it, usually, the thought that a man would rather stay away than come home and deal with her demands, complaints, or suggestions will drive even the most mild-mannered woman into a rejection fueled rage. There are people who get enraged at the thought they aren't the most important factor in their mates' lives.

When it comes to the physical act most men are at a loss, and the reason why can be summed up in a question; "Who teaches you how to be a good lover?"

Another of the many challenges Black men face is the subject of lovemaking. Black guys really have it rough in this department because of the psychological pressures established by society. Old myths like "all Black guys are well-endowed" cause many brothers to overcompensate materially from the fear of inadequacy. Almost all Black men dread learning that his partner may have had a bounce-around with another man, and if we find out that the person who persuaded our love has larger genitalia, for some reason it makes the betrayal even all the more painful.

I admit, at one time or another, I have questioned my own size, ability, stamina, etc. after a woman told me that not only was she done with me, but had also found another guy that was packing more than I was.

For some strange reason, some people equate sexual skill to the size of the guy's penis, the amount of time it takes for him to reach orgasm, the variety of the positions he attempts, or his inhibitions or lack of them.

When it comes to sexual satisfaction, some women prefer length, some like width, some like it aggressive, some like it slow and gentle, the point is women reserve a right to a preference, where men aren't allowed that luxury.

At the risk of sounding overly misogynistic, men can have an attraction to certain body types and parts, e.g. Tall and busty, long legs, etc. but we have no control over the size of the vaginal canal. If the woman has experienced several childbirths, hysterectomies, or any of the other different invasive procedures that involves a woman's pubic area, the resulting cavity may never regain its original dimensions, elasticity, and so on.

In other words, woman can find a dude with a twelve incher relatively easy, whereas we could want a vagina that fits like a baby hand squeezing your index finger, doesn't necessarily mean were even going to get it. If a man has a small penis he's just shit out of luck because he can't get smaller vaginas outside of becoming a pedophile, and I don't suggest that.

This is one of the double standards that I have an issue with when it comes to sex. It is almost as if I should be honored when a woman allows me the pleasure of penetrating her, and when this honor is bestowed upon me then it behooves me to be enthusiastic, appreciative, and attentive, whereas all she has to do is be there. The best way to describe it is, a woman laying waiting for the man to come and pleasure her, and the entire time not doing anything to reciprocate, then having the audacity to be angry when the man doesn't act as if he was just struck by lightning. There are way too many women who think they are doing you a favor by having sex with you. Although she isn't the only person there, some women think that their presence is the most important during a romantic rendezvous which in turn, makes some men resent them and treat them bad.

Where do you learn to be a good lover?

Does one get educated in technique, timing, and the rest by looking at porn, romantic comedies, tv?

If there is no healthy discussion, how does one learn about erogenous zones, subtlety, and seduction?

I believe we spend a lot of time listening to other people's fantasies when we ask them for advice sexually. It seems like everyone is convinced they are some consummate Casanova and capable of conquering and taming even the most fiery of lovers.

I haven't met a person who was content with being inadequate, boring, stiff, or uncaring and cold, most have resigned to just "getting theres" after dealing with selfish, entitled, or just unsatisfying lovers and failed attempts to feel the earth move. This is the attitude that women encounter when men are so persuasive to have sex then don't bother to call back. It's a combination of judgment and deflection, men absolve themselves of moral obligation by convincing themselves this is a normal occurrence for a loose woman, and it's not the man's shortcomings it's the woman's being naïve.

In other cases, the men become disrespectful, despondent, or distant because he sees the woman's unwillingness to participate, or her inactivity during the act as selfish, a lack of interest, a sign there is another man servicing her needs, or a host of other issues rooted in jealousy or rejection. I have known many women who were afraid to tell a man exactly what she liked sexually for fear of judgment. She didn't want him to change how he acted, leave her, or see her as a whore, or whatever.

I have seen women who were more comfortable with going through the motions than exploring what it was that she enjoyed. My personal opinion is so many women get told how they should act and what should be important to them that they don't actually know what they like.

On the other hand, seems like the women who know how to please a man sexually, use her abilities like some sort of evil power. They know how to move muscles, or perform certain acts and they use the reactions they produce or promise of later favors against the man for their own benefit. There are no emotions involved, no regard for feelings or repercussion, yet these are the women who scream the loudest when they happen to fall victim to the same game they play.

A lot of times when men can see the unbalanced advantage given to women in certain situations, and realizing the futility in begging a self-serving woman for acknowledgement, appreciation, or affection, most men will go where they can get it easy as opposed to having to work for a reward that doesn't match the effort they put into it.

To put it in simple terms: "What you don't do another bitch will!"

This is a particularly sensitive subject for some because there are many men that have been killed, attacked, jailed, and psychologically scarred from comments made by angry unsatisfied former lovers. I have tried to understand why Black parents never seem to talk about intimacy, romance, or sex with their children beyond the basic "knowledge of the world" lecture.

As a young man, I can't remember even discussing sex, I remember it was more important for my family to know when I started engaging in it, but no-one seemed interested in telling me about it. I learned that babies were a result of sex, you can catch a bad disease and lose body parts if you had sex with the wrong person, but never why people still did it. See, I saw it like this, babies were nice and cute, but they made a lot of noise and cost a lot of money and if this is what sex gets you, but not everyone having sex had babies, so what was the draw, why was everyone so excited about it?

Nobody ever told me, but, I found out.

In our community, sex is a means to an end. Sex is a way to manipulate, congratulate, celebrate, or humiliate.

HOES

In the Black community, sex isn't always about love, lust, infatuation, or seduction, in most cases, it's used as a means to control your partner. There are women who have realized that sex can be also used as the ultimate weapon.

Whores, tramps, strumpets, women of leisure and ill repute, bust-downs, jump-offs, hootrats, runners, chickenheads, blockheads, sluts.

These are the nicknames for women who use sex as a means of negotiation. There is a reason why prostitution is called the world's oldest profession. Since the beginning of time there has always been "tricks", people willing to pay for a little "release". Although most women won't admit to having sex for personal gain, the ones who do are called by society at large or themselves, hoes.

No woman starts out a hoe, whorish behavior is learned or adapted. Many of these women have been raped, neglected, abused physically and emotionally, resulting in her low self-esteem, or emotional detachment.

As I have traipsed the various boulevards, back

roads, and side streets of America, I have experienced more than my share of women who could be considered more than just emotionally unbalanced. Many of the women that I speak of suffer the psychological scars of coming from abusive/broken families, unfulfilled promises from former lovers, and the disappointment that accompanies realizing many childhood dreams will never be realized. Many of these women also had the unfortunate luck to be raised by a woman with a distorted view of reality.

As much as I would hate to admit it, our women are hurting.

There are specific reoccurring traits you find in almost every woman that could be considered a loose woman, but the most obvious one is low self-esteem. These women are usually irritatingly needy, possessive, dramatic, and angry. It would appear this woman could be satisfied easily if she met someone attentive and compassionate, but more times than not, she wants someone to be her punching bag. For some strange reason, a large majority of the "loose" women that I have met all seem to think if you're not willing to accept her mental/verbal abuse you are not masculine, dedicated, trustworthy, etc. These are the women I would see in public interacting with others while displaying a nasty disposition, dressed in some tacky, overly-revealing, unattractive, get-up behaving as if she were the only sane person on the planet.

It's my belief that everyone should dress and express themselves however they see fit, and no-one should try to dictate how anyone else looks. The flip side of that theory suggests that also means I have the right to take your physical appearance into consideration as ultimately a reflection of who you are as an individual.

As much as we would like to deny it, we judge books by their covers all the time, and we all dress the way we do for a reason. I believe women learn fashion, cosmetics, etiquette, and essentially how to be a woman by imitation of the women they have encountered. I have heard many of my female associates say that their fashion sense, choice of make-up and everything else came from women they liked, respected, or saw as strong, beautiful, graceful and so on.

Women who were spoiled, doted on, overprotected, encouraged to outperform, and sheltered usually, were the main ones who did the craziest stuff to me. You think their backgrounds would suggest the foundation for a well-adjusted adult, but the personality that emerges is far from it.

In most of my experiences these women are selfish, bratty, manipulative chameleons that could switch personalities in an instant depending on situation and desired result. Ironically, these women were usually victims of their own games, as more seasoned and less caring players used them and brushed them aside with less regard than waving at a bothersome mosquito. I personally believe that the high rate of unwed Black women is directly related to what I call the "princess" complex.

"The Princess Complex" is what I call the behavior I see when I encounter the entitlement issues some of these women have. The women who suffer from it usually have difficulty empathizing with anyone else's plight, surprisingly, even if it mirrors their own. These women are completely self-absorbed, usually to a degree bordering on the delusional, as they are convinced they are "the cat's meow" and deserving of special treatment because of their looks, family name, wealth, figure, etc.

Having had more than my share of casual encounters, I can say in all honesty, that these were the easiest to deceive. All I had to do was pretend to be understanding, and agree that it was just a matter of everyone being "jealous of her". Just the rationale of a person convinced that someone else's envy of them was grounds to do some of the things I have seen women do to relatives, friends, associates, colleagues and strangers is awe inspiring in itself. How does a person become so self-absorbed?

I think it starts at home.

Just like with Black males, Black women and their mothers have a special bond. In some instances you can see the tradition of the matriarch passing time honored techniques to her daughters and the solidarity of their sisterhood. In others, you can hardly believe this is a mother and her daughter after witnessing the scathing insults, facetious retorts, unwarranted assaults, and unresolved animosity.

At the risk of enraging women please allow me to state an observation: Some Black women are harder on their daughters than they are on their sons. Black women are taught survival tactics from their mothers, be it the boardroom or bedroom most Black women are taught to be calculating whenever possible, deceptive when necessary, and resourceful constantly.

In contrast, there are those who become "best friends" with their mothers, only to find the "friendship" is in jeopardy whenever mommy's wishes aren't met. The mother usually punishes the daughter with "the silent treatment", threats to end financial support, or by showing preferential treatment to another to "show whose boss" as it were.

There are a great number of women who were never taught "how to be a lady" by the women around them. I have seen women teach their daughters to be manipulative and bossy, to have unrealistic expectations, and how to punish those foolhardy enough to resist her advances or ignore her demands.

It seems in the Black community we have more rules set for punishing misunderstanding and nonconformity, but none in place for rewarding patience, perseverance, or loyalty. Looking at the Black community, and including myself, sometimes I think we are an unappreciative mob, unable to empathize with the sacrifices made for us, unable to comprehend the magnitude of our responsibility to each other.

The indifferent, nonchalant, "use what you got, to get what you want" mentality is more rampant than ever, and young girls are more bold, and direct than they have ever been in my memory. There was once a time when casual sex was something that occurred with a specific type of girl, and certain acts were reserved for special circumstances, etc.

These days having a wild encounter on the first day, within minutes of meeting, is the norm, and if you happen to be old fashioned, or moving too slow, chances are you will be insulted, or treated as naïve, lame, slow, or just plain dumb.

I have observed women who would rather approach sex dispassionately from the fear of later rejection, judgment, disappointment, or abandonment, but in reality, they desperately yearn for true intimacy and commitment. If you were to sit down with a woman who has been labeled as a "hoe", or one who makes questionable life decisions you would be surprised at how many just want to be loved unconditionally, but are afraid that no-one would ever be able to look past her faults. It's difficult for many people to imagine being completely alone, much less the desperate need for acceptance or companionship that accompanies that mind-state.

In my opinion, this lonely sense of hopelessness that drives some women into believing the fantasy that the average philandering dickhead (pimp) sells to her. The illusion of being part of a bigger ideal, that she has significance in something being built, and that her participation draws merit. That is enough to lure some of these broken women, others look for inclusion, thinking that her sacrifice or willingness to degrade herself should be an indication of her love, devotion and dedication.

When it comes to dealing with these types of women men usually approach it from one of two angles: “You’re trying to get something just like me, let’s just exchange what we have and there’s no problem.” The harsh reality that goes along with this approach is, ”Ok, you don’t have the right to expect anything after the exchange, including attention, money, special or preferential treatment.”

Even the most callous of women get attached, and usually at an inopportune time because of misinterpreted gestures, gifts, advances from men who enjoyed the excitement of the illusion but unable to deal with the reality. For example, how many strippers have gotten involved with a regular to find out his obsession for her ended when she got off the stage, and if she desired to continue in the same profession then she obviously has issues, is just a common whore ?

The second approach: there are men who know that the average “loose woman” is really looking for the Julia Roberts Pretty Woman fantasy. The guy just wants to have sex with a woman he sees as sexy, exotic or whatever, so to present a picture of sweeping her off her feet and giving her the perfect life is the bait you use for that particular trap. Variations include: “You’re not looking at her like everyone else”, “You understand, if she just gave you a chance you would take her away and she wouldn’t have to be degraded anymore.”

After taking a couple of those with no payoffs, some women become hardened, uncompromising and bitter. Everything becomes amplified, every man is a scheming good for nothing liar, and cannot be trusted, and she begins to use her anger, frustration, loneliness, or disappointment as justification for her lack of sympathy, compassion, honesty, or fidelity. “Nobody cared when it was me!” is usually the sentiment thrown at me when I asked, “What did I do to deserve such hateful behavior?”

Too many of us use our own pain as a moral barometer, we avoid accountability with the excuse if we hadn’t been subjected to a particular injury we sustained then we wouldn’t do it to anyone else. I find it ironic how so many in my community “look for a villain” instead of accepting the reality, repercussions or responsibility of our choices and actions. There are great amounts of women waiting for Prince

Charming to ride up on his strong and valiant steed when their attitudes and behavior would be more deserving of a bearded troll on a tricycle.

LISTENING

There are certain phrases that all men will hear at one time or another when interacting with a woman: "You never listen to me." The truth of the matter is, no matter how you react, chances are, you will still hear that sentence.

The best way to explain this dilemma is to use an analogy that I heard…

Women are moved by what they hear and Men are moved by what they see.

Most women even when given sufficient evidence to the contrary, can still be convinced to believe the most far-fetched notions, claims and assertions, if the suspect packages the falsehoods in compliments and praise. Men know this and exploit it to increase the number of conquered victims to boost his ego. If you were to ask any random guy in the street what is the key to successful communication with the opposite sex, I am quite confident a large majority will agree with me when I say having the ability to act, and give the appearance of listening and being interested.

In my own defense, let me remind the reader that not only is this a general fact among the male populace, it is a reoccurring theme in commercials, sitcoms, movie plots, and so forth. It has been my experience that a well-timed “uh-huh” “yeah” or “really” was enough to rescue me from the frustration of trying to understand what this woman was rambling on and on about. Usually the woman didn’t want an objective point of view from a neutral party, they wanted someone to listen to them bitch and complain, share their anger, and to commend them while berating and insulting the offending party.

You want me to listen to this madness, tell you how right you are, and how stupid the other chick is? Like most men, I don’t do that.

When we hear what is sure to be the beginnings of some dramatic tale of betrayal, fury and planned revenge, we will use any means at our disposal to escape. This mindset is the justification for some of our adulterous affairs, lies, and dumb decisions, the reasoning bcing, “I ain’t going home, I don’t want to hear that bullshit!" As I said before, men are stupid, and sometimes our indiscretions and rationale cannot be understood by those lacking a penis, or the maturity of adolescents. Instead of ending the dreaded relationship most men will continue to maintain an illusion of committed devotion out of some distorted sense of obligation, the excuse normally amounts to; "I didn't want to hurt you."

I have tried to sever ties with women amicably many times only to be accused of being heartless, emotionally repressed, manipulative, calculating, and worse. We hear all the time how simple it is to end a relationship, but rarely do we hear how to deal with a woman unable to let go.

I once wrote, "some women are looking for men to do what the last man wouldn't." It has been my experience that women are usually trying to heal wounds of old relationships with new ones. As evidence to this statement I present the following examples:

The battered wife looking for the gentle man who would never lift a finger to a woman.

The betrayed woman looking for the dedicated one woman man.

The aspiring executive looking for a man with drive and ambition that matches hers.

The single mother looking for a “real” man willing to provide for and protect her and her family.

In each one of these examples personal responsibility is dismissed and we are forced to assume that these individuals are deserving of what they wish for. In other words, how many battered wives have been the instigator and or antagonist of the assaults? How many women that have been publicly/privately humiliated by revelations of adulterous partners have been guilty of being negligent, unappreciative, or abusive themselves? What about the success driven female? Is it not safe to assume that people who are obsessed with personal achievement rarely have time for anything else? This leads me to the single mother.

At the risk of sounding like a typical misogynist, in my opinion, single mothers have gotten away with murder for years. Social programs, housing, governmental grants and funding, even the judicial system are unfairly balanced in favor of single mothers. I am by no means trying to minimize the difficulty of raising children without assistance, I am simply stating that some women use that reality as a crutch. No child deserves to suffer, but, if I may be so frank to ask, why do these mothers get off scot-free?

There are too many women exploiting the system to count. Women who continue to produce offspring irresponsibly with no regard to how the children will be provided for, just the assurance that the state welfare program will offer a set amount of assistance for a number of years. I have met, dated, and interacted with welfare moms from several states and I saw the same thing most of the time; complacency.

These women were essentially waiting for "Prince Charming" to ride in and save them. A noble and wise man to whisk them away from their depressing environment and immerse them in a world of luxury. Most of these women delude themselves into believing this possibility and become obsessed with superficial beauty, disregarding the needs of children. The kids' needs are pushed to the back burner because mommy needs to look good to get them a step daddy.

I have been guilty of being indifferent to the needs of women as I develop into the man I'm becoming. Convinced of my own self –righteousness I remained uncooperative and distant as women begged for my attention, believing I was worthy of more than this woman was willing or capable of providing.

In short, was a real dick.

"I don't have any kids, why do I have to deal with your drama?"

I wasn't guilty of impregnating a woman and leaving her to bear the responsibility alone, so therefore, I shouldn't be held accountable for the needs of the family I just happened to become involved with. Another demented theory: you have kids already so why can't you fuck me? These selfish sentiments mirror the apathy many men share when dealing with single mothers. She couldn't make that other dude care or handle his responsibilities, how is she going to give me demands and ultimatums? To me and other men that have thought this way at one time or another, a single mom was a guaranteed thing, having to spend a couple dollars to keep her rug-rats pacified was part of the battle. Any man that has dated a woman with children has made this adjustment, and will admit to it if asked.

With that said, let me inform you: there are two kinds of hoes.

1. BACKDOOR HOES

AND

2. HOES IN DENIAL

BACKDOOR HOES

A backdoor hoe is one of the most manipulative, conniving, deceptive creatures on this planet. She can be compared to the Black Widow spider, the one notorious for devouring her mate after sex. The backdoor hoe is a master of disguise and usually strikes at your most vulnerable moment. She pretends to be a close monogamous friend that is only concerned for your well-being, meanwhile praising all your virtues while simultaneously berating anyone she sees as competition.

When dealing with these types of women the ploy is usually to surprise you with a declaration of unwavering love for you. In this the man feels obligated to go ahead and get with the girl who is seemingly the perfect catch, feeling fortunate for having come to his senses in the nick of time to appreciate this treasure of a woman standing before him.

Wrong dummy.

Actually what happens is you give this woman ammunition to kill you with. The woman is usually some self-conscious soul who knows you would never give her a second look, but in becoming your "cool female friend", she learns all the mistakes the other women are making and knows what buttons to push, what to say, etc. She also may use her "inside info" to alert other females to any infidelity or secrets that may be being kept. All the while, maintaining an innocent "I have no ulterior motives" stance.

They come with gifts; offers to help with financial problems, clean houses, cook meals, baby sit, whatever the angle they can use to become a part of your world will be utilized.

For what?

Control.

The power in being a backdoor hoe is how she plants her seeds. If the man comes from a broken home family and loyalty may be extremely important, so appearing to be focused on the home and performing like a housewife, the man gets suckered in by his desire for stability and belonging. In return for her giving him what he needed, the woman gets a loyal man, she never has to worry about, if he acts up, remind him of who was there when everybody else left. A child will up the ante with most men and the love for this innocent child will deter many from approaching the relationship from a rational perspective when problems occur. Most disagreements are never resolved, simply swept under the rug for the sake of the greater good, (shut up, if she gets too heated she might keep your baby from you.) There are a lot of us who become bitter, hardened, and apathetic to the world after having been in one of these mind-numbing, masculinity stealing relationships. Imagine being confined yet being told how appreciative you should be for shelter. This is the type of madness many men deal with.

These are the women that remain in the background, sometimes for years, waiting for the opportunity to step in and become the perfect partner and assume her role. Men have been falling victim to this tactic for years. Women who hide behind this disguise all display the same general characteristics. They will appear selfless and unconditionally loyal and supportive, willing to go to the ends of the earth to assure that any and all needs are met, but the reality is, she's plotting.

Men are basically all the same, and we are creatures of habit, this is why we tend to attract and date women who cater to our essential needs and desires. The calculating woman knows this, and be it subconscious or blatant, in some way or another will attempt to exploit it.

I am not implying every woman who is assertive or has initiative is some up to some diabolical scheme with evil machinations. I'm simply stating some women realize that certain behaviors have similar results with a variety of men.

I have difficulty understanding why people won't acknowledge this fact. There are women who believe having the inclination to or performing particular domestic tasks should guarantee them a successful relationship. As a man, I appreciate a woman who has learned how to be a good housekeeper, but, that doesn't mean that's all I want or even need from a woman. I'm not speaking of the woman who was raised by an "old school" mom and taught caring for her family is most important.

I'm talking about the posers.

These are the women who are inclined play the victim, and more than willing to share all the heartbreaking details of her unreciprocated love. It's a tear-jerking tale of a woman denied the happiness that she deserves, desires, and has longed for. This uncaring, uncompassionate, insensitive jerk of a man committed a series of unforgivable offenses against this gentle, generous, treasure of a woman…

Her monologue starts with a sigh, an air of desperation and defeat, imagine Scarlett O'Hara standing in front of a large bay window with the back of her hand to her forehead in the "woe is me" pose. If only she could find a "good man", a man who knew how to treat a good woman, a man that knew which responsibilities to assume, a man who would accept all she had to offer. This woman never seems to portray a role of accepted responsibility, she never seems to have any fault or part in her failed relationships, it was always "what he did". It's always the same song, just a different chorus and orchestra playing in the background

If you listen to R&B music, especially anything popular from the last two decades, you will discover how much the victim mentality affects our collective psyche on a whole. He can't love you like I can, which is nothing more than the shallow boasts of some superficial asshole that believes material possessions are enough to compensate for lack of emotional fulfillment. Another popular motto: You are going to miss my love, which is code for: you took what I provided for granted, now regret it as I flaunt my newfound independence in your face.

These self-absorbed songwriters irritate the hell out of me. Love is cheapened to just a display of gift giving and ego stroking, what you feel for someone willing to compromise their morals and principals and comfortable with going bankrupt satisfying unnecessary impulses.

Nowadays, love is money.

HOES IN DENIAL

These are the women that have a long history of being promiscuous, yet have convinced themselves they aren't like those "other" women that sell themselves. They are actually worse. These women will usually get naked for the first person showing an interest in them. In addition to poor judgment, these women are often plagued with inferiority complexes and to compensate for what she lacks in confidence will cause controversy or "drama" as a means to get attention. In my experience, women like this have been the root of problems since the beginning of time. Remember Delilah? She is a classic example of a hoe in denial.

A hoe in denial has no problem jumping from bed to bed or man to man. She has no problem sharing secrets between enemies, revealing plans, or sabotaging goals, her main concern is "feeling" loved, wanted, or accepted. Rarely do these women take accountability for, or, look at the effects of their actions. Anyone unfortunate enough to be caught in the wake of her madness is at fault. Hoes in denial often use their emotions as justification for their selfish behavior.

"He made me mad!"

"I was tired of him so I…"

Ultimately, Black men can identify a hoe quickly. She is usually the woman willing to do anything to get attention. When we are looking for a quick sexual release, or cheap ego boost, she is normally the first choice. Her disregard for her own welfare, body, or self-image makes her easy to manipulate and persuade into compromising situations.

This also is basis for her expandability.

The average man believes that once he convinces a hoe into performing he must be willing to get rid of the woman or maintain the illusion; i.e.

spending money, time etc. Most Black men don't have the patience or resources to keep up the charade, usually these episodes were ones based on opportunity rather than plan. Most women who are considered hoes tend to have a twisted sense of loyalty, and are dedicated to the person paying them the most attention.

When you consider the fact that no matter how much you were to invest in this woman, the slightest error on your part could result in the most bitter of betrayals, most men opt to have their moment and brush the woman aside. She isn't dependable, trustworthy or reliable. The ridiculous self-serving logic being; if she were a good chick, he would have met her under different circumstances.

I'm sure you've heard the expression: "you can't turn a hoe into a housewife."

RELATIONSHIPS

It seems as if we have all been tricked into believing the same myth: there is someone for everyone. Recent estimates indicate that our population on Earth has surpassed 7 billion living souls. In the most ideal of situations one would be led to believe that it's equal opportunity for everyone to find a suitable mate, but reality says otherwise. Let's examine some of the factors that people seem to discount when they make these ambiguous sweeping statements.

THERE IS NOT SOMEONE FOR EVERYONE

"There is someone out there for everyone."

This is one of the most insane, immature, and irresponsible assertions that has been consumed and adopted by society at large. The mere fact that people buy into it reflects the general sense of delusion and entitlement that influences a great number of people from all walks of life. In my opinion, some people have allowed the unrealistic and highly romanticized rants of the lonely, insane, and desperate to impair their ability for rational thought.

Simply put, there are more women than men, how could there possibly be someone for everyone? In addition to this most obvious of facts, there is also the issue of class, race, age, sexual/religious practices and preferences, etc. When coupled with the other social/economic differences it's easy to see the inevitable problems this line of thinking will produce. There is a whole world of people that are inclined to believe that not only is their perfect match out there, but with all the love songs, romantic films, internet dating sites, and poetry that saturate the marketplace, many believe that their mystery love was created and bred exclusively to satisfy their every desire.

Most people believe that they are "good natured", they follow the rules of etiquette set by society at large, they do what has been labeled as "the right thing" by the general public, and they meet the expectations placed on them by friends and family, colleagues and associates. These are the people that are empathetic, and generous, they feel sorry for the unfortunate and they donate time, money, materials, and support.

These same people never stop and consider the fact

they are perhaps operating from a sense of superiority, and maybe they are insulting others with their self-righteous attempts to clear their conscience.

Having been in situations that required me accepting help from outside parties, on more than one occasion, I offended the individual offering help by refusing what they were offering.

I believe, at one time or another we have all portrayed ourselves as the sacrificing martyr, we were only trying to help, who is this person to refuse? Another facet of the "martyr syndrome" as I call it, is the need to berate and judge the person after they reject us, "they should be happy somebody was trying to help them!", or "I don't know why they acted like that, if it was me…"

In all our wisdom and benevolence, most of us never consider that the person we are interacting with has a list of intangibles that influence and determine their reactions and decisions, like past experiences, upbringing, fears, limitations and so on. We are so busy trying to do what's best for them, or show them how much we love them we forget it's not always about how we show our affections, but more times than not, it's about how these actions are being interpreted.

One of the most dismissive things that I've ever heard was; "I don't know why you are acting like that…" That's the point, it isn't you, and people forget that. We all have complained about the difficulty one experiences trying to find a suitable partner without realizing that we spend so much time trying to figure out why others won't submit to our will.

I read once there are three phases of a relationship:

INFACTUATION

POWER STRUGGLE

ACCEPTANCE

From what I have seen, there are a lot of women who lose interest with a man after the initial attraction stage. They enjoy the excitement of a new relationship, the anxiety and nervous energy of a first date, first kiss, and first sexual encounter. There is an old phrase that defines this type of behavior as "in love with being in love." These women like the attention and the fact there are no problems or complaints being aired. Everything is perfect and this is where some want the relationship to stay, unrealistically thinking that a good relationship never endures moments of hardship or disagreement. Women who operate from this train of thought all seem to share the same sentiment, when it starts to feel "regular" they have got to go.

The Black community is over-run with the results of women who acted emotionally or impulsively, namely, the abandoned and abused children, many who were produced as a means to keep a man involved, or as an ill-conceived display of a self-conscious woman's misplaced dedication. There are women who foolishly believe that guilt-trips and ultimatums are the solution to a troubled relationship. They essentially push a man into the proverbial corner and are surprised when the man attacks or defends himself like most animals.

For some odd reason, we all seem accustomed into shaming a person into being in a committed relationship with us, and the most common tactic is childbirth. Some use the father's participation as a sort of morality/emotional litmus test, his reaction and behavior being the scale to measure his loyalty, resourcefulness, resilience, or his capacity to handle responsibility.

A common misconception is if a man is caring, loving, or committed then he will make all the necessary sacrifices and changes to reassure the woman that he is in fact a good and supportive man. But, if and when the fantasy ends, usually after "Mr. Perfect" has moved on to greener pastures, some of the "love children" produced catch the brunt of the frustration, anger and rejection that is typical in a break-up. The person responsible for the injury is not available so it's common for many to attack the person that reminds them the most of the perpetrator, and sadly, it's usually the children who weren't really wanted in the first place.

Another problem is the woman who wants "to be a man's mother". These women look for specific qualities, like low self-esteem, desperate and needy, neglected or abused men, to be with. They don't necessarily want to save every Black man in the community, they just want one who will be appreciative of what she has to offer and in turn, be obedient and dedicated because she was the one "who took a chance" with him. That's a problem waiting to happen.

Women who enter the situation with ulterior motives rarely see the magnitude of their actions, or the selfish aims that motivate them. To them, they are the more honorable woman deserving of far more than the average for her attention, intentions, and actions. Most of these women have low self-esteem and need the validation she believes a relationship provides.

Others assume that if they provide an open supply to the things the man wants, like creature comforts, sex, money, etc. then the man is obligated to "act right". When her gifts or behavior doesn't produce the desired results, some women resort to insults and guilt trips to reinforce the thinking, "I gave you what you wanted why can't you treat me like I want to be treated?"

The thing that boggles my mind, is that many of these women are convinced and insist they were right, well-meaning, or the best choice for someone and completely overlook the fact that they had a plan to attract and seduce and romance someone.

I have learned, most people get upset when they find out they were manipulated into a choice they made not have made under different circumstances. Examples are, people who get taken in scams by con –men, people who get tricked into purchases by fast talking salesmen, people who become the victims of the phony psychic, spiritual advisor, the major factor being manipulation or mishandling of their trust. The things she offered become more important than anything else, and is the foundation for any ill feelings that may follow.

“I did so and so for him.”

“I gave him…” etc.

Another harsh fact, people will almost always take what they need without regard for how it makes the next person feel. A homeless man who hasn’t eaten in days may take you up on your offer of a meal or a warm bed, but is he a bad guy if he doesn’t want the relationship you had attached to the bargain? Does that man stop being hungry or in need because he doesn’t want to be with you? So why does one need to consider your offerings as anything beyond a means to solve a problem? Because some women refuse to think, and some can't see past their own desires. Some women will envision an entire scenario, complete with all the man's reactions and comments, how beautiful the future will be, and haven't said one word to the man she has her attention on, it's more of a case of "He better be ready when I come!"

To keep it completely simple, some men see the game, and exploit it. They see what's coming or expected, and do enough to reap the benefits they desire, and leave when the situation becomes too challenging. Everyone has a limit to what they will tolerate and accept, but some women think men should always be receptive and co-operative, even in the most ridiculous or stressful matters. It's this obligated, entitled, mentality that most men hate, and we use as fuel to drive some of the seemingly heartless choices we make.

Sometimes we try to play a game just to find out sometimes the game plays us.

I have never claimed to be an authority on any matter, much less relationships, but from what I have observed, most relationships fall apart as a result of the power struggle. This is the phase in relationships when the future of the couple is examined. To me, this is the time when you get to know who you are dealing with, their true personality, how they see the world, also most importantly, what they think of you. The power struggle is the phase when two people see the positions they are going to assume for the unit as a whole.

The questions could include but aren't limited to:

Who will be the primary money manager?

Who will be the tactician?

Who will be dominate/submissive?

Who will be the caregiver?

Who will be the breadwinner?

Who will be the homemaker?

Who will be the disciplinarian?

To me, people break up because they don't always want the jobs assigned to them.

Some men don't like being put into the role as rescuer, because he becomes responsible for averting any disaster, financing any impulse, and solving every problem. Some men resent the implication that as a means to or a result of interacting with a particular woman, he has to assume some responsibility, or provide a solution to a pre-existing problem, usually at the expense of his self-worth.

There are countless men who have had their manhood measured by someone's selfish expectations.

"If you was a real man..."

"If you really loved me…"

We have all been taught that true love is measured by a person's willingness to submit, sacrifice, or humiliate themselves for us. The harsh reality is, no matter how you see yourself, how noble your intentions, regardless of who you are, where you're from and the rest, no-one owes you a relationship.

I have yet to experience a situation where the duties or expectations between a woman and myself were clearly defined. Most of the time, my responsibilities were assumed and implied by my gender, or personality. For example, if it was a dirty job like working on a car or manual labor, then it was mine to do, if it was something that required money then it was my job as a man to finance the plan. If I suggested that the woman is capable of doing some of the less strenuous activities, like garbage disposal, then somehow it was interpreted as a reflection of my lack of respect for my partner. "I'm a girl", "I can't do that, I've never been asked to do that before." Etc.

As a man, I felt insulted that I could be relegated to certain activities on the fact that I'm a man, but women reserve the right to pick and choose what they will and won't take part in regardless if it's the norm, popular consensus, or common practice.

Believe it or not, this particular subject is the principle that motivates many men to become so contrary, argumentative and closed down, unable to communicate. There are men who are opposed to being controlled on any level and realize that with many Black women, compromise is not an option, but mandatory if he desires anything meaningful from the woman. I'm guilty of being invasive, abrasive and verbally abusive when I found myself at the receiving end of some woman's unreasonable and oftentimes unrealistic expectations. I will assume that I speak for many men when I ask, "Bitch, you do you think you are?"

Relationships aren't hard, we make them hard. You would think paying attention, being affectionate, and sharing secrets and ideas, would be easy to do. We all seek acceptance, validation, and appreciation on some level, so to give it should be a no-brainer right?

Wrong.

As I stated before, we as a people have a tendency to claim our rights as an individual at the expense of others. Many times we can find ourselves as the loudest voice in a mob of disenfranchised, bitter, angry, misguided folks who all share our gripes, sentiments, and dreams, but none of which has actually accepted their responsibility in the scenarios they are complaining about.

The definition of acceptance is easy to understand, but sometimes it deviates from what it may appear to be. In some cases, it can be looked at as "settling" or defeat. The acceptance phase can be seen as the catalyst for the couple's survival. In those instances, people decided to get along for the sake of the relationship or children, or people who thought it better to just compromise to avoid future arguments, or people who realized and appreciate their differences.

I have found myself inspired by, or in awe of those couples who had been together for a number of years and essentially survived the "test of time." I, like many others, sat in judgment and self-exalted approval of a union I had no information on. I just sat there smiling like a moron, day dreaming and fantasizing about what I saw as the ideal couple and wanting to have the longevity I ascribed to them.

To me, they had it figured out, they were the example of love when it works, and became the unofficial spokespeople for" relationships and how it's done". I never stopped to think what if they were acting? I never took into consideration that maybe one of the two had resigned to just being in the situation but no longer emotionally invested. I actually tricked myself into believing that at a certain age, people stop lying to themselves, or matured, dropping selfish habits and tendencies, but we know that this isn't the truth.

People are who they are, and more times than not, not who we want them to be, and in my opinion, this why people get so up in arms when a "respected" member of the community commits an offensive or criminal act. We give people power over us when we elevate them to positions of authority, celebrity, or importance. We transform them into god-like beings, incapable of wrong-doing. We fashion these people into external expressions of ourselves, our admiration of them becomes their moral prisons, since we have invested in them emotionally, financially or otherwise, they have the burden of having to be saints while we reserve our right to fail, falter or fall short. It's this disillusioned mind-state that immobilizes us and limits us from truly experiencing life and the joys of it. We allow ourselves to be restrained by the fears, desires, and demands of others, which in my opinion, makes things worse because broken people break other people.

The main point of this chapter isn't to shake anyone's faith, or to be overly pessimistic towards matters of the heart, but rather share some thoughts about how we impose our desires on others, and offer perspectives many may not have had an opportunity to consider. Whenever we allow ourselves to fall into the thinking that we are owed some sort of romance because of what we deemed as respectable or beneficial about ourselves, essentially we are stating that we deserve love because we want it, and that others have an obligation to perform a certain way because "they" know how we feel.

Ironically, the people who suggest that another person is inconsiderate, or unworthy of respect and decency because of an inability to submit, are usually the ones who have the biggest problem considering anyone else's feelings.

To sum it up, minds and relationships are like parachutes….

They work better when they are open.

COMMUNICATION

I have had a lot of arguments with Black women over what could been seen as the most petty of subjects. The most frequently repeated issue was my expectation for justice being ignored. I like most Black men, would like to believe I'm fairly easy to speak to granted one isn't attempting to "pull a fast one" on me.

Having seen the darker side of human nature, I find myself unable to tolerate some people's perception of reality. I don't try to turn anyone to "the dark side", I simply enlighten them to the fact that the happy, sunshiny version of life they occupy disappears once they enter my realm of influence.

I like to think of myself as a pessimistic realist, a firm believer in Murphy's Rule: whatever bad can happen usually will. I would like to believe in the goodness of people, but after witnessing countless atrocities committed with no explanation, provocation, or regard for repercussion, I learned, we are only as bad as we see ourselves.

This is how I see communicating with a Black

woman. Time and time again, I have attempted to resolve a dispute, air a complaint, or to convey an idea only to find myself screaming at the top of my lungs about something that wasn't that important to me. I like many other Black men, have been led to believe that our women don't respect us. In most of my past relationships communication always deteriorated behind my refusal to submit, or agree.

Why?

I saw it as control tactics.

My definition of an argument is pretty simple: two people trying to be heard and no-one is listening. In my opinion, even the most vicious debates can be solved easily when all sides, events, and reactions are considered, but it almost never happens in a Black couple's disagreements. Usually peace is reached when one or both parties involved dismiss the event or label the fight a stalemate.

This doesn't help the situation. Getting along to get along is one of the most irresponsible and impersonal conclusions we have adopted as a people. It instantly minimizes everyone involved in that it exalts physical interaction over actually getting to know a person. When you get along to get along, you essentially transform an individual into a position or a facilitator, their existence becomes a means to an end, like a father staying involved for the sake of the children, or a couple staying together to minimize expenses and maintain appearances with family or the public at large.

One of the more common facets of an argument is the "understand me first" approach. This is a result of an individual's inability to compromise. People that suffer from this selfish line of thinking find it impossible and impractical to consider anyone else's feelings before theirs. These are the people who find it necessary to stress the magnitude of the offense committed against them, how it made them feel, and the ripples caused from it, however they find it difficult to understand anyone else's position, perspective, logic, or reactions. These same people are ones that propose their approach is more significant, meaningful, or practical, and after they have laid out their specific argument there is no need for any more discussion. Men deal with these know-it-all types and develop a severe distaste for conversing about anything beyond normal day to day activities. When a woman suggests that she and her man need to "talk", some men become overwhelmed by the anxiety and sense of hopelessness they experience.

Although there are many of us who would do almost anything to establish an open line of communication with our significant others, we are faced with the reality that it may never happen. Another issue that prevents us from progressing as a unit: the "justified payback". People who operate from this mind-state feel that anger, rejection, disappointment, or previous misunderstandings are license and validation for any and all reactions.

"Now you know how it feels!"

I have a serious problem with these types of people. Perhaps it's the self-righteous air of superiority, maybe it's the fact these people have taken the liberty to be disciplinarian of the world, whatever the underlying principle may be, I detest people who assume they have the authority to reprimand or punish someone for behavior they deemed as inappropriate.

I have said before, there are some Black women that believe they are above judgment, scrutiny, or correction. These are the same ones that spend a large amount of time reminding you of every mistake you ever made if you ever make the error of mentioning any of her shortcomings. People like this feel threatened by confrontation or exposure and will fight tooth and nail to not be labeled wrong, selfish, or uncooperative.

Women who have this issue usually are callous, manipulative, or downright deceptive because her self-worth is measured by how she appears to everyone else around her. She is more concerned with maintaining her image than her relationship, and when faced with this type of self-serving woman, many men realize that there may not be a possibility for a better more positive future.

We then start trying to find qualities that we can substitute for what we see as personality flaws.

"She ain't a conversationalist, but she can cook…"

"She gets on my nerves, but the sex is amazing…"

In theory, this type of relationships doesn't sound too appealing, but believe it or not, there are more people involved in this type of pointless, destructive union than one could imagine. People seem more content with finding someone to “just be there” and to have sex with regularly, than someone they can actually build and grow emotionally with.

Some Black women have picked up the capacity to “like who likes them”, whereby they try to create a substantial relationship with whomever is available. This causes problems on a number of fronts; namely, the person who was “accepted” can develop feelings of resentment, rejection, or hurt once it occurs to them that they weren’t necessarily desired, but allowed to enter a woman’s life. The man could begin to feel “played”, disposable, or insignificant, especially when he begins to consider that he wasn’t exclusive and that his current position could be filled by anyone.

Some people may be comfortable with being “second choice”, an afterthought, or the back-up plan, but like myself, there are a great deal more that are vehemently opposed.

There is an old saying: speaking is the lowest form of communication. In addition to this is the different psychiatric and scientific conclusions suggest that human communication is more body language than actual verbal exchange. If you wanted to see a practical application of this theory, just sit around a Black couple during a disagreement.

Admittedly, we are a passionate people, and in some cases understandably so, but in all honesty, we take a hell of a lot of undue liberties with each other under the mask/defense of "we were being emotional". In my opinion, the Black community resorts to the "sympathy card" a little too much for my liking as I have witnessed numerous accounts where someone avoided repercussion, punishment or been rewarded after they turned on the tears or pulled on the public's heartstrings.

Albeit idealistic philosophy, my opinion is unjust rewards create unjust works. As is often the case with people who are able to get by deceptively without exposure or accountability, they end up paying a greater price at a later time. Not everyone gets his come-uppance publicly, but as taught by Napoleon Hill in Think and Grow Rich, one concept in universal law states compensation always seeks it's source. I do not want to begin a metaphysical discussion on causality, but rather, offer some spice to a conversation that will undoubtedly get heated on occasion.

When I was a young man, I was told repeatedly that something was wrong with me because I verbalized my displeasure with situations and people. I can vividly remember being told by several different people that being outspoken or defensive on my own behalf was a bad thing, or something that indicated a deeper hidden issue.

"You're talking like a chick…"

"Are you gay or something?"

"Men don't talk about stuff like that…"

One would think those are quotes from different males right? All of those comments came from women, and more importantly, family members.

As I stated in an earlier chapter, the wide majority of Black men today are, and were, raised in a fatherless home. As a result of this, many Black women had to attempt the impossible and try to teach boys how to become men. Without adequate knowledge of men beyond her experiences with men, many women are ill-equipped to provide what is required to teach a man how to be a man.

To make matters worse, factor in a bad attitude from a failed relationship, financial problems, entitlement issues and any other random issue you can imagine and the entire situation intensifies. Beyond housekeeping, money management, hygiene, etiquette, and self-preservation, there is not much more a woman can teach man, especially in regards to how a man is supposed to think. That is not to imply women cannot teach a trade or a skill, but a woman cannot teach a man how to "be" a man.

When a woman educates a man about dealing with women, in all honesty, she only has a couple of perspectives to draw from. In my opinion, she can only teach the man in question certain things to do, behaviors and clues to look for, and mistakes to avoid. She usually approaches the situation from her recollections of happy or sad times, or, fond memories of past and deceased family or friends, which is, essentially, making a clone of another man she deemed as good.

No matter how a woman tries she cannot teach him how to think masculine, how to control his male urges and thoughts, she can only plant ideas rooted in her own likes, dislikes, and limitations based on how she believes he should cater to a woman.

Most of the Black men I know were reinforced with a deep rooted fear and dependence on "momma". Without positive men to help us establish a male perspective, or a strong sense of identity, purpose or direction, a lot of us guys stumble through the world observing as some maladjusted female would, hyper-sensitive, sometimes unreasonable, always expectant.

Since the majority of us were raised by women who could be seen as rigid, untrusting, and distant, unknowingly, some of us have adopted the mentality and philosophy we saw the most, mommy's.

"This is the way my momma does it."

"My mother doesn't make it like that."

Most people place their mother as the most important if not the most influential person in their life. Understandably so, as she was often the force behind almost every little milestone we reached. Every accomplishment from the mundane and trivial, to the things we considered as monumental, it was almost a sure thing, you could almost always count on Mom to be there, encouraging, supportive, dedicated and loving.

That's a beautiful picture isn't it?

Too bad not everyone can envision it.

Some people see or hear the word Mom and they drift off into fantasy land, relishing sweet memories of knowing without a doubt that they were loved, appreciated, and that someone cared for them no matter how bad things got, Mom was always going to be Mom.

Some people hear the word Mom, and it conjures dark and disturbing images, of pain, abuse, neglect or abandonment. There are people that don't get nostalgic at the sound of the ice cream truck, people that cringe when they hear children laugh. There are people who have a negative physical reaction to certain situations, people who hate to be touched, as well as people who hate crowds, and so on.

The point of mentioning these people is this; no two people will see any situation exactly the same way. This fact seems to go out of the window when talking to some Black women. I can't count the times I tried to explain to a woman how unfair she was being by insisting that other people should listen and submit to her feelings. Most of the time the woman would raise all kinds of hell about how unfair the situation was to her, and more importantly, if people were open-minded enough to allow her to voice her opinion, the situation would be easily and quickly solved.

You know, in my opinion, there is nothing more insulting than some simple ass person suggesting that whatever I'm going through is child's play when presented to the computer that is their mind. To add insult to injury, the things they are begging to be allowed into the discussion usually never have a damn thing to do with the original debate.

There are a lot of women that believe they are the "solution". These are the women who always seem to have a personal stake in the matter at hand. These individuals usually are involved, excited, overly-enthusiastic, not knowing their presence and attention is, most times , unwanted and unwarranted. These women act as if their knowledge of a situation is all the grounds they need to get involved; they are the significant other, they are an important family member, they have been around, they care the most, they gave the most, etc.

Communicating with these types of people is hard enough, with their entitlement issues, feelings of obligation or resentment, etc., but when you add in the unwanted help, advice, remarks, or reactions, things can get out of hand quickly, and, in a major way.

There is a popular belief that men don't like to talk about their feelings.

This is partly true.

Men don't like to talk about their feelings… to women.

It's been my experience that no woman ever thinks she can be irritating, selfish, unapproachable, or difficult to talk to, and, if you attempt to tell her, be prepared for a verbal onslaught of monstrous proportions. Any insinuation that she isn't the most delightful, insightful, joy to be around that she may think she is will resort in her taking the liberty to remind you of your flaws, and that you should appreciate your good fortune in that she even gave you one bit of her precious time, spirit, and energy.

In my short time on Earth, when presented with this scenario, in almost every instance, that type of attitude was usually met with a robust "fuck you Bitch!" Perhaps I should broaden my circles.

I can only speak for myself and a few others that I have discussed this topic with. Every time we began discussing the things we found the most frustrating when interacting with our "Sista's", the one thing we all seemed to agree on was the nasty, argumentative, inconsiderate demeanors a lot of our women have started to display. I listened while we all told the same story but with different details, trying to find a solution to a problem but never getting a chance. We all could relate to the frustration a man feels when engaged in the "circle argument".

The "circle argument" is what I call the argument that goes on and on because one person if too focused on placing blame and one person is deflecting. It doesn't start like a "circle argument" it starts as a disagreement or observation that one person has and the other sees as offensive or insulting…

"Why did you do that?"

"Why did you think that?"

Even though the question could have been based on sincere curiosity, or meant as a humorous nudging, sometimes our emotions get the best of us and we misinterpret and act inappropriately. You know, we get all insulted and say something equally hateful back to them? They/We respond in kind with something we deem as insulting or embarrassing , they react, we counter…this is what makes the conversation go in a circle. The original topic is lost, and now the discussion becomes a competition and comparison of disrespect.

"How can you say something like that to me when all I asked was..."

"Well, you know how I felt about that, so I said…"

As a man, one of the things I learned a long time ago was I cannot win an argument with a woman.

Not because I have lost every one I've ever had, not because she was more vocal or had a better way of articulating her thoughts. It was not because she somehow convinced me she was right and I had to concede.

I and a whole community of Black men have come to KNOW that we cannot win an argument with a Black woman because, she won't let us. A man can have waterproof theories, philosophies, evidence and irrefutable witness testimony. It still doesn't matter, because there are some women out there will not admit they are wrong, mistaken, or misinformed under any circumstances. You could try to approach the situation from a variety of angles in an attempt to elaborate on your feelings, this usually will cause the woman to start deflecting anything mentioned to her, and overlooking your rights or needs as a human being.

ALL MEN ARE DOGS

This is one of those general things that imply a host of things, but accepted as fact, popular opinion, and reality for all. In an attempt to show a contrast, consider the old saying; "it's a woman's prerogative to change her mind". I interpret this cliché as a society wide accepted validation to excuse an impulsive choice by a woman regardless to consequences or who it may affect.

All men are dogs implies that men are inherently predisposed to a particular mindset and set of behaviors, in my opinion, which by definition could be interpreted as the determining factor that separates us from the more superior, civilized, controlled woman.

I have reluctantly come to the realization that my focus on things of a romantic, sentimental, or emotional nature will be analyzed, and interpreted as homosexual or some sort of psychosis if I mention my "feelings" one time too many. Men are told to "man up" when seen in a vulnerable state. In many neighborhoods, Black boys are taught that crying or showing emotions is soft, gay, or something to be ridiculed, because men don't cry.

In our community, males are taught to separate themselves from emotion to show courage, strength, tenacity, or maturity. I have heard many a woman speak highly of the man she was fond of, and on more than one occasion being thrown off when a woman said she loved a man for never raising his voice.

I would like to think that I am an open-minded individual. I try to look at things from several angles and make reasonable choices, assessments and conclusions. I believe, to extoll the virtues of a soft spoken, repressed, or emotionally disconnected person is sheer insanity. The reason being, the people that say these things usually haven't taken the time ascertain why the individual in question is so quiet. I base my conclusion on one factor: the person who praised the behavior would have to have had some experience with the opposite side of the spectrum to determine which they prefer. Therefore, praising someone for not doing something that you have a problem with is ridiculous.

Everyone responds to yelling differently. Some people feel attacked, some people ignore it, some people feel threatened, and some people cry. No matter how you feel, your reaction has been developed over time.

Ironically, the most harm done from yelling comes from the volume of your voice, not necessarily what is being said. In a heated debate some women are threatened by the animated and erratic movements and gestures, the contorted facial expressions, the facetious and abrasive vocal tones. Men are taught that some women don't like loud confrontations, that's why we often approach gentle and reserved, the main aim: to gain your confidence and reassure you that we aren't some psychopath looking to slice a chick up.

Men are always at the mercy of society's rules, and most of us will be on our best behavior as long as we can, or until we just can't tolerate a situation any more. Most of the time, we will be at our wit's end trying to find a way to not offend the woman and she will do or say something that causes us to see red.

If the woman is overly self-centered, or unreasonable, she will have trouble understanding her partner's frustration and mistranslate their irritation and anger as signs of an abusive personality, immaturity, or just an unnecessary overreaction. That's why women are so shocked when "Mr. Perfect" loses his mind one day over some trivial matter. I share a problem with many men, I hate repeating myself or mentioning the same thing more than once, and if you're ever in a relationship with some of today's Black women, you then know, sometimes you will have to repeat yourself consistently.

Another disturbing element I have noticed, some Black women's inability and refusal to empathize with anyone else. I am not suggesting that all Black women suffer from this, but there are a great number that do.

It has been my experience when engaging in a discussion with a woman of color, it's better to suspend reality than to approach the matter in a mature, responsible, or adult manner. In my many failed attempts at a monogamous relationship, I have oftentimes found myself at the receiving end of a psychologically destructive verbal barrage that would have almost certainly led to suicide had I not been as thick-skinned. Black women are unrivaled when it comes to the art of demoralizing a person, and no topic, personal issue, or experience is off limits.

I am not implying that men are better communicators, in all honesty, most of us are terrible at articulating our thoughts and intentions, we men usually resign to just doing an act and hoping for the best. A man could have sincere romantic intentions when offering a gift, but some unappreciative women will complain about the man's presentation, his lack of attention to detail, the amount he spent, where the gift was purchased, etc. Most people give gifts to convey certain sentiments: a show of love, celebration, and congratulations, to memorialize or commemorate an event of importance, no matter what the reason, more times than not, a gift is meant to extract a reaction, influence a decision, or to repay a debt.

We have all heard "it is better to give than receive…"

"Don't look a gift horse in the mouth…"

I'm sure a lot of us have all been taught that we should be appreciative of anything given to us from another, and we all have been unconsciously put into a state of obligation by someone else's generosity at one time or another. Personally I don't like the idea of "submission by proxy", when someone does something for me and is expectant of a comparable response. This is a control tactic that most men I have known despise.

A better way to explain would be: a woman performs certain acts, or makes purchases with the intention to obligate the man into remaining in the relationship or exhibiting particular behaviors, and are usually upset when things go contrary to her plan.

On a side note, many of the women who try to manipulate a man into living with her under her rules, would never enter into a situation where the man was the dominate position. These women cannot deal with a man who is their equal financially, her worth is instantly diminished, and without her possessions to flaunt she has no power.

Add all these random components together and you may begin to understand why some Black men are apprehensive to discussing particular subjects with their mates. In a general sense, a lot of us feel unappreciated, unwanted, and undeserving of a real relationship. We have been told on different occasions that we shouldn't vocalize our complaints, our fears and conclusions aren't legitimate, and, had it not been for our woman's momentary lapse in judgment, we would have never been considered as a candidate for a relationship.

In a way, it's almost as if you are being assaulted without provocation and your attacker telling you that should be grateful they are attacking you, and that is for your own good.

I would like to say that most Black women are good listeners, but the reality is, not so much. Black men, including myself, have adopted the "need to know" mentality. We have categorized out lives into situations, events, and information that our women "need to know" or "don't need to know."

Things that would be listed under "need to know": age, birthday, family history, sexual preferences, etc. These same things could be listed under "don't need know", and looked at as a defense mechanism because men don't always know the true personalities of the women we date. As a result, we choose the things that we deem as relevant or pertinent to interact with a person and the rest becomes classified and kept secret. I believe it comes from the moments of embarrassment a man feels when he realizes that his woman is unreasonable, disloyal, or inconsiderate of his feelings. Most men I know prefer companionship to being single, familiarity over random encounters, and problem-solving to endless debates.

While learning how to maneuver through the world, I have adopted the philosophy it is better to discuss a problem openly instead of ignoring the issue or dismissing it. It has been my experience with some Black women, they would rather deflect blame or avoid the situation altogether, so becoming apathetic seems like the most reasonable conclusion.

In summary, it's not that we do not want to have better communication with our female counterparts, but for many of us, after many failed attempts and different approaches, we have resigned to doing what it takes to get sex, companionship, or a family. I think it is because we have learned often painfully, that what we want and what we're going to receive aren't always going to be identical.

Who would continue to explain their feelings or desires after constantly being minimized?

There are some Black women that don’t think that anyone else experiences feelings of rejection, or frustration. They cannot comprehend the damage they inflict on others mentally, financially, or otherwise, so time is wasted anytime anyone makes an effort to get through to them or appeal to her sense of decency. These are the spiteful, sarcastic, bitter women that always seem to have a remark to make, an axe to grind, or an excuse for what they’ve done, but cannot fathom why they are single and why anyone else would have a problem with them.

There is truth is the saying “men don’t like to discuss their feelings”, but, in reality, ask yourself this: if you were always told your feelings weren’t valid, warranted, or up for consideration, how much would you want to talk?

HONESTY

In the Black community honesty has more than one definition. In most cases, honesty is meant to imply complete disclosure, no detail being overlooked or discarded. In other cases, namely Black relationships, honesty is relative to the amount a person is invested emotionally.

There are people who believe that everyone should be completely forthcoming about all events and thoughts that occur during a relationship, while others believe some things should be kept secret and only revealed after all else fails.

When dealing with some Black women, some men experience instances where honesty is defined as any information that the woman may deem as harmful. In these cases, the woman suggests that withholding certain information is equal to telling falsehoods, the logic being, anything that is hidden must certainly be of a negative nature. These women have convinced themselves that a man who is willing to reveal his vulnerable side is ideal, but these same women usually use any knowledge gained as leverage, or a control tactic. These women use one sided moral arguments to guilt trip a man into confessing his darker secrets. Refusal to participate is considered blasphemy and an indication that this man is unwilling or unable to commit because of a deeper character flaw. This tactic is effective because most men, as I stated previously, will do almost anything to get out of a heated argument and “shut this girl up”, as it were.

Many of us don’t like the idea of disappointing our mates, upsetting them, or doing or saying something that may result in a break-up. Most men are reactionary, many more impulsive, and most times we do what we think is right for the moment without any foresight or consideration of harm. We don’t always think about the results of our actions, or who it may effect or how.

If you asked the average man why did he cheat on his woman, most of the time you will hear a confused “I don’t know”. We are victims of our egos, and most of our indiscretions happen as a result of it. Truthfully, most men don’t realize why they do the disloyal things they do, and most of the transgressions occur because of opportunity rather than malicious intent.

Simply put, some men cheat just because they had

a chance to, not because they were legitimately interested in someone else. I know individuals that have destroyed marriages, lives, and households because they thought they found the answer in a newfound attraction. The contrast in what they receive from the "new" person and the old relationship being the deciding factor. Most people misinterpret the excitement of a new relationship as having found something better. They celebrate and rejoice this "new" union without realizing the only real difference is the "new" person has limited knowledge, if any, of the past relationship, and doesn't exhibit any of the behavior that influenced the choice to look elsewhere for romance.

In situations like these, one person may decide that revealing the nature, history, or existence of another relationship may be devastating or hurtful to the other person involved. When presented with the choice to break someone's heart, or soften the blow of a break-up, some people think it better to omit certain details, package the disturbing message a particular way, or, outright lie to avoid an emotional exchange, argument, or losing some benefit they gained from the "old" relationship.

In other cases, there are some who think that there are times when it's easier to give someone a "sanitized" version of events than actual facts. They reason, it's better to let them down easy than be brutally honest, because the person has assumed acting this way will spare their former love of any extra pain.

Having been on both sides of this particular world view, I can say with confidence some things don't need to be said. After having my world rocked by a revelation and being told all the ins and outs that occurred, I have found myself confused and wondering what was wrong with me. I would have been better suited to deal with a callous dismissal than someone telling me how frequently she ran off to have a secret rendezvous.

I'm more partial to being left confused. I really don't care to know what it was that I did to spark this type of retaliation, as if knowing were some sort of special provision being made for me to not make the same mistake again.

Black women have a tendency to do things like this often. Not only is the situation your fault and she was just a hapless victim, most will get upset if she senses that her explanation isn't enough to dissolve any anger you may be experiencing. You don't have the right to be angry because if you had done something else or handled things differently, this wouldn't be happening, and you wouldn't have to witness her show of disregard.

More times than not a humiliated man is reminded repeatedly his woman isn't responsible for any pain he's feeling, she is justified in her actions because of her needs as an individual, and essentially, "you brought it on yourself".

The thought that someone owes another person more consideration than themselves is laughable to me. I have seen women that have nagged incessantly to get their way from their partner. Be it his limitations or fears, principles or standards, I have seen women that have insisted that her man wasn't suited to be in a relationship and underserving of anything emotionally fulfilling or substantial because he refused to compromise his beliefs. There are women who don't want what they ask for, they just aren't accustomed to being told no, and if they are ever denied anything, will go to the ends of the Earth to make sure she gets what she requested.

I made a startling observation some time ago: it seems as if some people like being lied to. We all have the same need of acceptance and validation from time to time, but some people seem more receptive to fantasy than fact. This is evidenced by women who have been offended when told the truth at uncomfortable times. A woman can feel apprehensive about a garment she purchased or wants to wear, she can say she wants a genuine critique, but after getting it, most are offended, insulted, or incredibly, angry that you didn't lie to her.

The reality of this situation; these women usually reach the same conclusion, feel the same way, or have a similar idea , when their fear is validated, then the other person is guilty of not understanding ,or being ignorant, uncaring, or, uninterested. An overweight woman usually knows she's overweight and physically unattractive to some men, but these same women will adopt the stance they should be afforded the same opportunities as other women. It's almost like they have the right to be desired, and even if you don't like overweight women, one should be more open-minded and willing to give a person a chance.

The most ironic thing, the same theory doesn't' apply to them, they have the right to decide who they interact with, they can refuse any man for any reason, but you're not a real man if you can't look past her flaws.

This self-exalted mentality, I believe, is what draws such negative attitudes from some Black men. There are many assumptions and expectations placed on a Black man before, during, and after dealing with a Black woman. The greatest of these is to never undermine a Black woman's importance, authority, or presence. Of all the misconceptions we have about our difference in gender, some women believe that constant criticism of her man is akin to showing concern. These women are convinced that their advice is infallible and priceless and one would have to be a fool to not take her suggestion under advisement and duly noted.

For a lot of men, living in a fantasy is the alternative to being alone.

These men have "settled", and accept the ridiculous demands and observations thrust upon him. These are the men forced to sit and hold their tongue when their partner is giving themselves undue praise, or berating another woman from a self-righteous perspective. They sit in amazed wonder as some overweight woman psychologically analyzes another and suddenly solved the mystery of "the reason so and so has gotten so big!"

I have personally witnessed women who were poor housekeepers admonishing another woman to "clean her nasty house up". I almost found the audacity displayed as unsettling, until I considered the source.

These are women who live in their own reality, a reality that is void of any influence from any outside parties. These are the women that cannot take any statement at face value. They take it upon themselves to investigate and disseminate statements made by everyone else, because, they think that no-one else is capable of being genuine or as honest as they are. These deluded ladies need to be convinced of an individual's innocence, contributions, or sacrifices, and will use any excuse to justify her invasive and disbelieving nature.

I have a few unpleasant memories of how insulted I was when I discovered a woman I confided in had went behind my back to verify my story. To me, it was calling me a liar, nothing more. I realize that there are a lot of dishonest manipulative people from both genders in society, so I understand someone being distrustful even inquisitive, but when someone is checking the veracity of some trivial situation I described, that is my opinion, a bit too much.

In those situations, it has been my experience that the person is looking for a reason to judge you.

They may or may not have formulated a particular opinion about you and need some information to make a conclusion. You may have omitted some details from your version of the story. There may another explanation to the situation that you have failed to reveal. Whatever the reason, these people by definition fashion themselves as the last bastion of truth, the upstanding and morally just person of unquestionable character, you're just another lying man.

With those things said, allow me to present another theory: we are only as honest as we need to be.

When a man meets a woman, it usually starts with a physical attraction, although women know this, we still have to pretend that we are looking for substance as opposed to a one night stand. The fact that we live in a society that is superficial and mostly illusion directly contradicts peoples so called desire for truth and honesty. Women coat their faces in make-up to look different, dress a certain way to appear sophisticated, professional, sultry etc. and then have the nerve to say they want to attract a real man. They walk the streets in disguises and costumes but contend no-one takes the time to discover and appreciate the "real" them.

I, like most men have wondered, with all the overly emotional reactions, unrealistic expectations, and nonsense that a lot of these women cause, create, and carry, why do so many believe that they are an ideal match, and much less, worth of the unswerving devotion they craze?

The truth is, some men would rather the one night stand, but if you say that's all you want, most women get offended, and you won't get it anyway.

In my opinion, honesty to some Black women is merely a device to get her man to see things from her perspective. Most Black women that I have interacted with seem to think they never make mistakes, and when they do, it's the man's responsibility to be mature, diplomatic and understanding.

One of the more common abuses of honesty I have seen; the "if you love me" tactic. This is when a woman uses guilt or shaming tactics to get a man to admit to something she suspects, or to get an appropriate response.

In other cases, the woman will use "if you love me then you should be able to tell me", the man goes for this trick in an attempt to connect, bond, or resolve a dispute, only to find out he would have been better off by avoiding the issue as he had been doing.

In almost every other scenario, honesty is subjective. A woman may say she wants your honest opinion about something, but the truth is, usually she just wants attention or praise.

Again, I do not wish to upset anyone with my insights or observations, I am simply articulating some things that are apparent to some and not so much to others. In my opinion, there are a lot of us that are incapable of being honest with ourselves, let alone someone else. There are those of us who are self-conscious to a fault, overly critical and hard on ourselves for what we see as weaknesses. There are even more still who don't want to be reminded of their faults, mistakes, or poor choices. We seem content with filtering out the behaviors, traits, and attributes of ourselves and others to get what we need.

Sadly, when people fail to meet our expectations of them, it seems we are more focused on the other person's refusal to maintain the illusion than our inability to shatter it. We all want the satisfaction of knowing how attractive we are, praise and acknowledgement of our talents and achievements, but most important of all, with all our imperfections someone that see us as perfect.

So the question I pose is: is it really a case of

wanting honesty? Or, is it more that we want someone who is considerate enough to know when or when not to lie to us?

ABUSE

In my short time on this planet, I have been both victim and victimizer. I have responded violently in situations that required a more delicate touch, understanding and patience. As a man I can admit that we often overlook the underlying issue in our attempts to command respect and as a result, many women have been left wanting. There is no justification for physical violence, and of all the excuses one can find, they usually require some sort of validation from others. Any man I ever heard recount his involvement in a domestic situation seems to try to get others to empathize with his actions, or the results thereof.

"What would you have done?"

"You think I'm wrong?"

"She had it coming right?"

I once asked a woman who I had been violent with: what was it like to be hit by a man, and how did it affect her? I know most people would consider that an offensive question, but I am not like most people. I believe in order to get know someone it's important to have an idea how that person thinks and interprets the world.

The incident with this woman occurred during a stressful time in our relationship when communication was all but non-existent. I had expectations that I felt weren't being fulfilled, I jumped to certain conclusions, I overreacted. In retrospect, the reason why I acted the way I did was caused by my fear of being dismissed, replaced, or not being seen as dominate and worthy of respect.

For most Black men, our possessions or finances become our identity, and we overcompensate for our lack of substance. We are programmed to believe that certain occupations, achievements, and social status will guarantee us the luxury of being seen as more desirable, but the truth is often quite different. Many of us have been misled to believe that our resume entitles us to certain privileges, perks and benefits, because a woman should feel honored to "have a man like me".

From this perspective, women become obligated to perform the way we instruct them to. If you are living in the lap of luxury at my expense, many men believe, your only focus should be satisfying my every desire.

To me, this is an after-effect of the focus placed on materialism and personal wealth in the Black community. As I said before, many of us are taught from birth that money is the solution to every problem. Some men never really find out what they truly enjoy out of the need to maintain appearances, "do the right thing", or go with the flow. There are too many of us that are in relationships, living arrangements, and families that in all honesty, not where we want to be.

In a great number of these situations, the man remains out of a sense of obligation, loyalty, sympathy, or fear of change. Some men cannot accept feeling defeated and develop feelings of resentment for the woman he has committed himself to. For these men, violence towards their partners comes from a sense of righteous indignation, his actions justified by his own assessment of his contributions or sacrifices. He believes that his woman's appreciation should be displayed in certain ways, and when she fails, then he has the self-appointed right to "correct" her behavior.

Domestic abuse has become a water cooler talk topic, a subject that sure to draw audiences as evidenced by the countless talk shows, mini-series, and programs dedicated to approaching the effects and damage suffered by the victims. There have been times that I have found myself screaming at the television in frustration over what I saw as an unfair amount of attention focused on the victim's assault rather than what caused it.

I believe that our society has been trained in to shaming a person into conforming to general consensus or popular practice instead of educating people on how to interact with one another. If a man doesn't understand the wrong in what he has done, punishment or reprimands don't help the situation. What I have seen, in most cases, the man is berated and insulted, informed that he is a coward and that he should learn to appreciate his woman. Sometimes the woman is instantly absolved of any responsibility in an altercation if her wounds from the attack are extensive or cringe inducing, even if she was the aggressor.

I am guilty of being a misogynist at times, insisting that the man's side of the story should be taken in to account to make a fair determination of who was to blame, at fault, or take responsibility. If I happened to be in the company of a woman most of the time I was reminded that I wasn't being empathetic to the woman's feelings, or "what she was going through". I heard that on so many occasions that I detested seeing any program that portrayed a woman as a victim. Like many men I saw all women as manipulative, scheming, deceptive tricksters, and if a man hit a woman, there must have been more to the story.

When I asked my female acquaintance what was it like to be hit by a man, she got extremely upset and I wondered why did it seem like such a pivotal moment? To me, we had a fight that got heated, I did something I regretted doing. I didn't understand when she started to speak about her shock, disappointment in me, how her perspective of me had changed, how vulnerable she felt, etc. I was so intent on trying to let her know that my actions weren't malicious but the result of misdirected frustration, I didn't realize the real damage weren't the blows but all of the mental pain that follows. All those times I couldn't relate to the victim on the program were the times that I was justifying my own immature behavior. I couldn't understand it before because it didn't affect me or anyone that I cared about.

As I said before, it is my belief that we as Black men, measure ourselves with superficial, material, and insignificant criteria. We foolishly believe that material possessions, titles, or money determine our worth and desirability. When we encounter some of the combative, argumentative, and confrontational attitudes displayed by Black women, many of us feel challenged, threatened, or emasculated. Disagreements become attacks on our ego, as some women act as if ignoring the problem, or bringing up an older issue will defuse the situation, when that doesn't work, they will resort to personal insults, name-calling, etc.

Black men have been taught that fighting is the last course of action when in an argument, but when all else fails, just beat his ass. When dealing with a

Black woman, most of us assume that our partner shares our experiences and knows the unwritten rules of the street, Black culture, and survival. There are a lot of men that have seriously injured a woman for crossing the line and questioning his manhood, ability to perform, or even suggesting that he was lacking in comparison to another man. I have seen enraged women in the heat of the moment completely say and do some of the most shockingly disturbing acts in a search for revenge with no regard for witnesses or repercussion.

The ironic thing, both sides of our community uses society as an excuse.

Black men have often been cast as the victims of endless persecution. Although the advantages of White privilege are apparent, I feel as if we defer to the obvious prejudices that exist a bit much when in many instances it's not the machinations of some diabolical conspiracy, but rather our lack of focus, direction, or foresight that limit us. Racism does still exist, but our insistence that all problems that befall us are a direct result of it, is in my opinion, a weak excuse.

It seems as if our community has been

programmed to find a villain to blame instead of accepting responsibility for our choices and actions. Perhaps it's a sign of my own hyper-sensitivity, but I am disgusted every time I witness someone Black operating from a deluded sense of entitlement. For example, the Black single mother complaining that the welfare system doesn't provide enough for her kids. Another example, the Black man who believes it's someone else's responsibility to give him a job, despite his appearance or lack of experience.

Too many times I have witnessed one of my contemporaries humiliate themselves when they vocalized their unrealistic expectations of society at large. In these instances, we take advantage of the public's sympathy and use the knowledge of the existence of discrimination and preferential treatment as validation of our complaints.

Some Black women have said they feel minimized and objectified by a system that caters to and rewards those with superficial beauty, perfect figures, and a willingness to please. After suffering multiple injustices, many Black women adopt a defensive stance, and the slightest transgression gives them license to use what they see as their only weapon, their mouth.

Since most Black women lack the physical strength and stature to beat someone into submission they feel their only recourse is to administer the verbal equivalent when upset.

"I'm a girl, I can't beat you. I can't do anything with you, all I have is my mouth."

"I just said some stuff out of anger, you didn't have to put your hands on me."

To me these comments speak volumes.

The first thing I gather from these statements, if she could, a woman would use her physical dominance to enforce her will. Since she can't, some women believe their only alternative is to be as destructive verbally as a display of strength, pride, and equality.

Abuse is a taboo topic in the Black community, as we all know, mental health and crisis counseling isn't a top priority in most Black households. There are many of us who are familiar with stories of women who were raped by male family members, males who were psychologically scarred by over-bearing parents, and no steps being taken to help the victims cope with the effects. The customary course of action is to ignore the problem, as if pretending the issue doesn't exist is equal to a solution.

From childhood, many Blacks are taught to avoid the perils of the world by threats of physical violence, guilt trips and ultimatums. Pain was the answer to disobedience, poor performance, or mischievous acts of rebellion. A child simply had to be reminded who was stronger, bigger, older, or in charge to eliminate any unacceptable behavior. This belief and practice is so wide spread and popular that many Black comedians have admonished and advised White parents that the disconnection between them and their kids could be bridged by "whooping their kids asses."

Black men have been on the receiving end of many of these misconceptions. For the most part, Black men have been trained to respond physically to emotional stimuli. I believe that Black men have been trained to measure the world from a testosterone based mind-set. We have been programmed to instinctively measure an individual's worth by material possessions, physical stature, and personal achievements. When one or more of these criteria is questioned or brought under scrutiny, our pre-designated reaction is to fight, defend ourselves, or provide evidence that we are in fact superior to whoever challenges us.

Abuse is defined as; the physical, psychological or sexual maltreatment of a person or animal. The illegal, improper, or harmful use of something. Insults.

From this definition, it's easy to see how many things can be considered abuse, but are they really? My conclusion, abuse, and things that are considered abusive are subjective.

Many Black men feel misunderstood, unappreciated, and outright disrespected in their relationships.

Human beings are naturally inclined to self-serving behavior; it's hard-wired into our genes through our self-preservation survival tactics. We all inherently seek the things that will bring us satisfaction, instant gratification, entertainment, etc. Black men have a disadvantage when it comes to this area of life, because so much of our identity is associated to, and derived from our achievements and possessions.

We have been trained to measure our worth and manhood by our cars, homes, salaries, and the appearance of our mates. A successful man was one with a beautiful woman, nice expensive automobile, and a fine home. Anyone who had less than this was considered a failure, not a real man, or lacking in other masculine traits. Although never formally announced, these are the primary motivating factors for many endeavors pursued by Black men in general.

When we meet a Black woman and a mutual attraction is established, one of the initial objectives is to present our future plans and our means to achieve said goals. Once we have indicated our intent, many Black men believe, at this point it's a woman's opportunity to participate or retreat. If the woman decides to associate herself with the man, then the assumption is, the woman will accept her role and act accordingly.

This is where a lot of the problems start.

In my experience, whenever I met a Black woman, our conversations usually began with introductions and explanations of why we were single. For some odd reason, I have noticed that people always blame the ex for the relationships failure. It is always the other person's fault: an inability to cooperate, unfaithfulness, a major betrayal, or another heinous act. We always seem to find a reason to absolve ourselves of any responsibility when it comes to our own heartache. After portraying ourselves as the misunderstood and hopeless romantic, we then try our best to maintain the illusion that we present.

Black men are notorious for living beyond our means and perpetrating a fraud to romance a woman. I could try to make an excuse for such immature behavior, but I am certain that it would be misinterpreted as justification for apparent and blatant manipulation.

Truth be told, many of us are desperate for companionship, and with all the stereotypes and unrealistic expectations placed upon us, the fact that some feel the need to be deceptive is understandable and a necessary evil.

There are a lot of women who have accepted the role of "victim" in her relationship. These women are the ones who are unable to separate themselves from their abuser for fear of violence, verbal abuse, or financial loss. I have encountered women who by their own admission were the causes of their unhappiness. They were the ones who initiated arguments, hurled the first insults, destroyed property, and over-reacted.

Many of these same women would resort to filing fraudulent police reports, recruiting outside parties, and public outcry to demoralize, incarcerate, or destroy any disobedient man. I am by no means trying to imply that there aren't any men who are inherently violent and abusive; I am simply attempting to present an argument that identifies some of the triggers to such behavior.

Some Black women complain about everything. There are some Black women that don't know how to be happy, no matter the circumstances. These women are never satisfied, and they feel the need to berate anything and anyone she feels deserves her attention. Black men get frustrated interacting with this type of personality because nothing we do is ever substantial, significant, or satisfactory.

These are some of reasons Black men will assault his partner. I realized that when attempting to explain my rationale for such immature behavior to someone I had injured, they interpreted my words as justification instead of an attempt to give them a clearer understanding of my thinking. Truth is, women don't care why you did it, but rather, she wants you to know how much it hurt her and your promise to never let it happen again. Trying to tell a woman why you hurt her is more offensive to her than the actual assault because most would like to believe that their man exalts them to a position above everyone else.

I have made the mistake of striking a woman. I say that it was a mistake not because I injured another human being, but after I considered everything that I affected by the action, I realized that it would have been better had I just walked away.

On the police report that was filed after one altercation, I saw how the woman's account of what happened detailed my actions, and portrayed her as the victim of a savage yet unprovoked attack. No mention was made of the comments that infuriated me or her insults; the focus was my imposing physical stature, destructive intent, and her fear of me. I marveled at how the arresting officers accepted her testimony as fact without investigation or evidence. Anything I said was instantly discounted as the lies of a coward, and I was threatened under the notion that I was only a bully and my true weak and defenseless nature would be exposed once I was introduced to "real tough guys" and got "punked out".

We always hear the stories of guys who were actually scared little boys who dominated their women because he was afraid to assert himself anywhere else. Nobody seems to think that "good guys" can lose their temper or do something irresponsible.

On top of this, there are many women that believe women and women alone deserve respect at all times, whereas men have to prove themselves. As Black men, we are taught to submit to and serve women at all costs, including the expense of our self-worth, self-image, and self-respect. Many Black men have been influenced to behave like children; dependent on the woman in our life to make all important decisions.

With so little to inspire us, it becomes difficult for many Black men to articulate the hopelessness we experience in our personal lives, and as a result, we become violent, abusive and apathetic. There are great numbers of Black men that share the sentiment; "look lady, I matter too!"

I am not always moved to quoting scripture, but one in particular comes to mind. In Genesis, we learn the story of the first couple; Adam and Eve, and God's instructions to them. They disobeyed God's commands and committed the first sin. After discovering the errors of His creations, God punished them saying: "you will bruise him in the heel and he will bruise you in the head."

When you consider the tensions experienced between Black couples in relation to this prophesy, one can see that it rings true. An angry Black woman can put events into motion that will immobilize a man, whereas a man's effect on a woman, the majority of the time, is purely psychological.

FAMILY

Family is more important than anything to some Black people, and many will sacrifice everything and do almost anything to provide for and protect their relatives. This by no means is meant to imply that other races don't have a deep rooted love of family. Blacks have been historically known as a tribal people, which to me, is the reason so many components of our culture have communal traditions, like house/rent/Block parties, Friday night fish fry/card game, etc.

I was born during the seventies when the social changes initiated by the civil rights movement started to take effect. Like most people, many of my fond childhood memories involved interaction with relatives and close friends. Isolated in our own universe, I can remember times as a child when I had gotten angry when some outsider threatened to interrupt our private gathering. It was simple: I loved the small circle that I was familiar with; anyone else being introduced into it threatened my relationships.

I, like many other people was brainwashed into believing one of the most significant moments of a relationship is when your partner expresses a desire for you to meet their parents. The sentiment was meant to convey a sincere interest for a committed relationship, but usually it was nothing more than a validation session. Parents scrutinize every facet of your person; upbringing, education, occupation, future plans, etc. The assumption being, they are just looking out for their child's best interest, but the truth is, they measuring your worth and resources to see how well you will provide.

We all think we know the individuals that we call family to a certain extent, but we really don't observe them beyond the role they play in our lives. It's hard for some to see their sister as some over-sexed nymph, or their brother as a sado-masochistic submissive sex slave, but the reality is, everyone have different tastes.

We all seem to look at our relatives with an air of selfish entitlement and expectancy, because of how we are trained to act towards those who have been identified as kin, or "blood".

Many people believe there are certain acts that are mandatory for all family members, including;

financial help in emergencies, emotional support and understanding at times of mourning, forgiveness whenever requested, and free babysitters without question.

There are some Black women that actually look forward to meeting her partner's mother, seeing it as an opportunity to cement her position as "the one", but it doesn't always turn out that way. I never did quite understand why some women assumed that they could get a better determination of who I was as a man by meeting my mother.

Our community's collective consciousness has been supplanted with notions that stem from ill-conceived and poorly conceptualized theories; namely, if a man doesn't respect his mother then he is incapable of respecting another woman. This is one of many ridiculous clichés that always seem to spring from the lips of some self-righteous broad trying to justify her judgment of a man's background or temperament.

In my experience, the person that my mother would like the most I would usually come to despise. I believe that we all would like to have a partner that our family welcomes with open arms, but we often forget, we as a people aren't as open as we would like to think.

What does your family do for holidays?

Do you gather at one another's homes, exchanging gifts, sharing meals and memories?

What church do you and your family attend?

What God/god do you believe in?

I ask these questions to illuminate a point: most people cannot truly empathize with others. From what I have observed, most people simply have things that they tolerate from others but never understand.

Religion is a good example.

In my relationships, although I may have told the women my upbringing and aversion to certain traditions and rituals, time and time again I had to make compromises from my partner presenting her faith to me.

Ironically, most of these women considered it beneath them to even acknowledge my beliefs much less respect them.

Having being raised a Jehovah's Witness and seeing the mass public's distrust and disregard for a religion that had been categorized as a cult, it was easy to see why women weren't eager to embrace my beliefs. There was a lot of misinformation and misconceptions about how the religion operated, what they believe and practice, and why they knock on people's doors.

It has been years since I have been inside a "Kingdom Hall", read any of the literature, or referred to myself as "Brother" Owens, but to this day, I still don't celebrate Christmas. Not because I still accept the teachings, rather I have discovered alternate doctrines and theologies that countered my initial beliefs and forced me to reconsider my position. Ironically, even with this knowledge you will be surprised how many times I have been penalized for not producing gifts during the yuletide season.

I don't go around broadcasting my beliefs to everyone, or educating them to the pagan origins of the Christmas traditions, but I have been reminded year after year how special the time was, how I was supposed to feel and act, and what the season was supposed to mean to me. Even after showing I was violently opposed to taking part in a particular celebration I was portrayed as just being unreasonable, uncooperative, or just irrational, not someone who was defending his morals.

Popular opinion dominates many things in the Black community, and we all seem to suffer from the "herd mentality" in one way or another. The best examples being our personal and choices and goals, most having being decided by our families and loved ones' advice, guidance, or demands.

We tend to do things that others are comfortable with to our own disadvantage, neglecting our own desires, needs, and expectations. We then use the limitations we placed on ourselves to impose limitations on others. We weren't allowed to do something so they shouldn't be allowed to. We were made to behave a certain way, so everyone else should have to as well. I believe this vindictive, unbalanced view of justice is the cause of many of the problems within the Black community.

To be completely honest, many Black men, including myself, have grown tired of having to be the mediator, goodwill ambassador, or facilitator between their partner and their families.

Somehow our romantic involvement obligates us to defend her interests, reputation, or property at all costs, regardless to fault or nature of the problem.

The “new” boyfriend/girlfriend gets sucked into the middle of an argument between siblings that is based on a long-standing dispute, what do they do?

First reaction when put in these situations; defend the person you’re with, because technically they are the only one that means anything to you. This usually makes the family members dislike you, the common excuses: you should have not gotten involved, you don’t know the whole story, its family and you’re not even guaranteed to be around any real significant time.

Something I found strange was some Black women’s ability to be callous to children. There are a lot of women that will have you believe that she loves ALL children when nothing could be further from the truth.

She loves *her* children.

I have seen numerous Black women that would knowingly disregard another woman's child if it benefitted her. There are women who will ask a man to ignore his responsibilities with a child that isn't hers, while demanding nothing less than the best for her own offspring.

Another facet to the family dynamic is the circle of friends your partner has. Many Black men find their women's friends to be worthless, catty, argumentative, instigators that aren't their friends at all. There is a factor that many people overlook; Black women hate each other. Countless times I have heard a Black women say they don't get along with other Black women, or that interacting with a group of Black women isn't the most appealing idea to them.

There are women who maintain a love/hate relationship with their acquaintances that men cannot understand. Yet, these are the same women who place their friends' opinions or suggestions above her partners, and allow outside parties to control their relationships. It's been my experience that the woman who is the most concerned with your relationship is either envious of it, or somehow feels threatened by it. On top of this, the women who seem to be convinced they know the sure fire way to handle a man are almost always single.

There was once a time when accomplishments by other Blacks served as inspiration for the generations that followed the pioneers, which in turn elevated the race. Now success is measured in dollars and profitability, character by popularity, and personal milestones are used to berate anyone not enterprising enough to match or surpass them. The greatest example of this is the family gathering, where siblings and relatives all congregate and compare goals and possessions and compete for the praise of the family as a whole.

"You know, he has a good job, he got married and bought a house. He's doing really well, why don't you get yourself together like…"

Individuality has been replaced with imitating, originality has been replaced by "remixing", just take something that was popular and reintroduce it with a slight variation.

"If I can do it you can do it" was once said as a

challenge to someone squandering his potential, now, it's stated as if to assert "I did it this way, and you should do it this way too…"

This is the most obvious when you look at how many desperate people resorted to drug dealing as an escape from poverty. Selling narcotics has become the no-brainer for anyone looking to supplement or create income. This is the destructive group think mind-state at work. Oliver Stone's remake of Scarface has been the inspiration for many would be drug kingpins.

People actually believed if you followed the main character Tony Montana's example, you too could live in swanky homes, drive the luxury cars, wear the finest clothes, and rub elbows with celebrities.

Some unfortunate brothers actually believe by repeating the catchphrases "Don't get high on your own supply", "First you get the money, then you get the power, then the women will come." or "Who do I trust? Me that's who!" , was all it took to become a drug lord.

As if the secrets to the underworld had been laid in a two hour blueprint.

Believe it or not, popular culture influences more than you would believe in Black communities. Popular opinion has been our weakness for generations, as fewer and fewer Blacks stand up in resistance to civil or social injustices. We have become a people more suited in playing the victim, than fighting. Seems it's easier to complain how unfairly we are being treated than doing something to change the conditions we whine about.

Another example is the recent media fascination and embrace of the pimp/prostitute culture. Pimps were looked upon as less than human for the way they objectified, manipulated, used, abused, destroyed, and then ultimately discarded the women they ensnared with their empty promises of glamour and excess.

Now it's cool to be a pimp.

Pimps are desirable, and looked at as sophisticated players who understand the deeper nuances of male/female interaction. They knew how to keep a woman in line, yet appear cool, calm, collected, and confident all the while.

Truth is, anyone slightly familiar with that way of

life knows that a pimp is usually a self-conscious, approval needing, parasite that was constantly worried about something, and hardly deserving of all this new found praise for his profession. This book is intended to shatter some misconceptions and introduce a new perspective, what Black men say, think, and ultimately, what is it that we want?

What does all of this have to do with family you may wonder?

We are products of our environment and the people within them. Some of us are making decisions, choosing mates, and living our lives for and through the approval of others.

Some of us do not realize that much of the life we choose, and ultimately the people we become stem from an action or inaction of someone else. An encouraging word from a parent has been the inspiration for many success stories in the world, and just as many failures have been associated with neglect and abuse. There are many people who would undoubtedly led different lives had they known someone was concerned for them, gave a kind word or expression of affection.

Ironically the people we invest the most into are usually the ones who yield the least in return.

When you think about it: it's all relative.

END GAME

I assume there will be a number of women who will skip to this page trying to get the answer to why we call you bitch. I apologize but it isn't going to be that easy.

As I said before, we hate the know it all type women who think of themselves as superior intellectually, as they always seem to believe that they can assess anyone and anything instantly. I attempted to share a variety of perspectives and opinions that Black men share throughout the chapters, and shed some light on what men think, and why we may react the ways we do.

If you haven't taken the time to read the few words I put together, I strongly urge you to go back and just take a peek at some of the perspectives I present, you might be surprised.

I mean seriously, the book ain't that long!

What is a bitch?

Would you not agree there are women who exhibit a "bitchy" vibe?

What do women call other women who flaunt their wealth, abuse their positions and or power, verbally abusive, selfish, controlling, over-bearing and demeaning? What do you call someone who is inconsiderate and needy yet demanding and controlling?

There are women that believe that they and they alone possess the right to insult, berate, criticize, or harass anyone at any given time.

"Ooh, look at her outfit girl, she looks a hot mess!"

If you mentioned to this same individual that perhaps her hairdo or outfit wasn't exactly flattering, no doubt she will be first to voice her right to adorn herself as *she* chooses.

There are women that believe that men are simply on earth to satisfy the demands of women.

There are women who believe that they know the best thing for a man despite the fact he may be opposed to everything she suggests.

There are some women who believe her intentions are comparable to solutions:

"I know things are rough for you right now, I wish I could give you a big hug and make you feel better"

As if a physical display of affection is enough to offset any stress you're experiencing. Or, the fact that someone is in an emotional state for you is equal to support or assistance.

What Bullshit.

The late comedian Patrice O'Neal once said: "Cheating as a man; sneaking out of your own house to go find some happiness behind your back, so your feelings aren't hurt. Cheating is for you, it's not for me."

He also said: "Secretly men hate women."

After presenting the obvious as well as the not so apparent issues that some Black men have, what conclusions can be drawn? Black men feel marginalized, emasculated, unappreciated, obligated, and disrespected.

Bottom line: we are sick of being manipulated.

Some Black women can never admit to being

wrong. In my opinion this is the primary reason why many receive the treatment they complain about. These are the women who usually have a list of emotional justifications for choices they have made, somehow their intentions are supposed to excuse immaturity or irrationality.

I have lied to, misled, and manipulated women, I have no excuses or explanations, point blank, I did it.

Like many of my brethren, I have grown tired of the customary rituals and nonsense that constitute being in a relationship. The sickening repetitiveness of certain conversations, outings, and situations, is what motivates many of us to conquer as many as we can in an attempt to salvage some sense of choice.

To many Black men, appearing to have a stable of women to choose from is more appealing than being with one and having no identity within the relationship.

There are some men that can ignore the damsel in distress.

There are some men that don't think you are as

irresistible as you imagine you are. There are some men that know you are full of shit no matter how much make-up you wear, no matter how tight your dress.

Yes, no matter what you do, there are some men that just don't give a damn.

For everyone who hasn't got it yet: I will explain it in really simple terms.

Women are moved by what they hear, whereas men are moved by what we see. For many Black men, when we call you names it's more our opinion of the behavior we see at the moment, not a sweeping indictment of your character.

In all honesty, when you really get down to the root of the problem, one thing we all must consider. Albeit destructive and unproductive as a word in any context, the problem really isn't what the man means when he calls you bitch, it's more a case of how you happen to feel about the word.

The conclusion that I have come to is we spend too much time trying to make everyone else happy and never truly exploring the things that will bring us true joy. This is by no means a suggestion to disregard others desires and needs, just a call for a little more rational thinking as our choices impact the race on a whole.

We are a people indoctrinated to believe that faith in scripture, unquestioning obedience, and submissive silence is the key to happiness, when all human achievement is rooted in a breaking of the rules, thinking outside the box, going outside the norm. We have to embrace our differences as individuals before we can begin to consider committing to one another.

There are too many clichéd scenarios that we re-enact day to day, too many rehearsed comebacks, too many regurgitated old-wives tales and isms that need to be eliminated. They usually start with; "if you ever see..." or, "if you wanna…" these are all control devices that we impose on one another to make ourselves feel dominate, important, beautiful, etc.

Why do we call you bitch?

Because we know it hurts you.

"WHY WE CALL YOU BITCH"

I.R.SMART LLC. NUTWARD ENTERTAINMENT

tackyrudevulgar@yahoo.com

http://www.blogtv.com/People?NUTWARD

twitter@Mr.Monstrosity

ISBN: 978-1-105-63610-3

www.ingramcontent.com/pod-product-compliance
Ingram Content Group UK Ltd.
Pitfield, Milton Keynes, MK11 3LW, UK
UKHW041944190726
13854UKWH00004B/1773

9 781105 636103